CONTENTS

INTRODUCTION

THE age of freezing has more or less eliminated the necessity to prepare meals according to the ingredients available for the time of year. However, in Britain the quality of our food is as good, if not better than anywhere in the world and making the most of freshly grown vegetables, fruits and other seasonal specialities when they are at their best and cheapest ensures a varied and healthy diet. Remember to look out for wild fruits too – elderberries and blackberries, for example. If you have the space to grow herbs (and it needs only a small window box or a few pots) why not have a go at nurturing some fresh basil or tarragon in addition to the more common parsley, thyme, sage, rosemary and dill? If you don't have a garden, or if you simply don't like gardening, then it's well worth being aware of ingredients which are in season so that you can plan meals around them before embarking on a shopping trip for more expensive foods.

Spring: home-produced lamb, new potatoes, asparagus, broad beans, spinach and turnips, French beans, mangetout peas, spring onions, spring greens, gooseberries and apricots.

Summer: salmon, peas, home-grown salad ingredients, courgettes, globe artichokes, beetroot, strawberries, raspberries, redcurrants, cherries and peaches.

Autumn: mussels, scallops, oysters, pheasant, guinea fowl, mallard, hare, partridge, pigeon, root vegetables (swedes, second crop potatoes and carrots, Jerusalem artichokes, parsnips), cauliflower, Brussels sprouts, leeks, blackberries, apples, pears and plums.

Winter: turkey, venison, cabbage, old potatoes, chestnuts, brazil nuts, walnuts, oranges, clementines, tangerines, mandarins, pomegranates and Seville oranges.

SEASONAL
Cookery

HAMLYN

Illustrations by Anthony Sidwell

Published 1986 by
Hamlyn Publishing,
a division of The Hamlyn Publishing Group Ltd,
Bridge House, London Road, Twickenham, Middlesex, England

© Copyright Hamlyn Publishing 1986

ISBN 0 600 32666 7

Set in 9½/10pt Old Style

Printed in Great Britain

—— SPRING ——

As the days get longer and the sun warmer the choice of seasonal foods becomes much wider. Leafy green and salad vegetables are abundant, the new season's home-produced lamb is tender and succulent and there is a wide choice of fresh fish.

St Valentine's Day gives an excuse for a romantic candlelit dinner and Beef Valentine followed by Coeur à la Crème is an ideal choice. Holiday Gammon makes an economical Easter Sunday lunch for a crowd or Three Pepper Chicken with Turnips is a delicious choice for a smaller gathering. Hot Cross Buns are easy to make and can be frozen if made a week or two in advance. Tangy Rhubarb and Ginger Jam is delicious as a change from marmalade for breakfast and Tea Bread makes a welcome tea time treat.

CREAM OF CARROT SOUP

675 g/1½ lb young carrots	salt and pepper
2 celery sticks	3 tablespoons plain flour
25 g/1 oz butter or margarine	300 ml/½ pint milk
900 ml/1½ pints water	3 tablespoons single cream
2 chicken stock cubes	chopped parsley or grated orange rind to garnish

SCRAPE the carrots and cut them into small pieces. Scrub and slice the celery.

Melt the butter or margarine in a large saucepan, add the vegetables and cook gently for 5 minutes, without browning. Add the water and stock cubes, season with salt and pepper and bring to the boil. Cover and simmer for about 30 minutes or until carrots are tender. Purée the soup in a liquidiser or food processor and then return it to the rinsed-out saucepan.

Blend the flour with a little of the milk to make a smooth cream. Stir in the remaining milk and whisk the milk mixture into the soup. Bring to the boil, stirring constantly. Just before serving, stir in the cream.

Serve sprinkled with chopped parsley or grated orange rind. SERVES 4 OR 5.

BAKED VEGETABLE SOUP

2 celery sticks	2 beef stock cubes
2 medium carrots	salt and pepper
1 large onion	½ small French loaf
¼ small, firm white cabbage	75 g/3 oz Cheddar or
2 tablespoons oil	Gruyère cheese, grated
900 ml/1½ pints water	

THIS makes a very substantial soup, ideal for lunch or supper.

Scrub and slice the celery. Peel and coarsely grate the carrots and onion. Shred the cabbage finely. Heat the oil in a saucepan. Add the vegetables, cover and cook over a low heat for 5 minutes, shaking the pan from time to time to prevent the vegetables sticking. Stir in the water, stock cubes, salt and pepper. Bring to the boil, cover and simmer for 30 minutes or until the vegetables are just tender.

Meanwhile, break the bread into small pieces. Place the pieces on a baking tray and cook in a hot oven (220 C, 425 F, gas 7) for 5 to 8 minutes, or until crisp and golden brown.

Put half the bread in a deep, ovenproof dish. Sprinkle with one-third of the cheese and then pour over half the vegetable soup. Repeat for the second layer and top with the remaining cheese. Bake at the same temperature until the top is golden brown and crisp, about 10 minutes. Serve hot. SERVES 4.

EGGS WITH WATERCRESS SAUCE

1 bunch watercress	4 tablespoons single cream
150 ml/¼ pint water	salt and pepper
½ chicken stock cube	4 eggs
40 g/1½ oz butter	4 small slices bread
15 g/½ oz plain flour	1 clove garlic

WASH and trim the watercress and chop roughly. Place in a saucepan with the water and stock cube. Bring to the boil, cover and simmer for 5 minutes. Cool slightly, then purée the mixture in a liquidiser.

Melt 15 g/½ oz of the butter in a saucepan, stir in the flour and cook for 1 minute. Remove from the heat and blend in the watercress purée. Return to the heat and bring to the boil. Reduce the heat and simmer, stirring, for 2 minutes, then stir in the cream. Season well and set aside.

Boil the eggs for 5 minutes and then plunge them into cold water. Remove the shells when the eggs are cool enough to handle. Fry the bread in the remaining butter until golden on each side. Cut the garlic clove in half and rub the cut sides all over one side of each piece of fried bread. Arrange the eggs on the fried bread.

Re-heat the watercress sauce but do not boil. Spoon the sauce over the eggs. Serve warm. SERVES 4.

POTTED CRAB

1 large crab	½ teaspoon salt
a little lemon juice	*To serve*
175 g/6 oz butter	brown bread, toasted
¼ teaspoon nutmeg	lemon wedges
¼ teaspoon cayenne	

PREPARE the crab or ask your fishmonger to do this for you. Remove the brown crabmeat and divide between four small ramekin dishes. Sprinkle with a little lemon juice. Remove the white crabmeat and flake finely.

Melt 100 g/4 oz butter in a small saucepan and add the white crabmeat, nutmeg, cayenne and salt. Stir over a low heat for 2 to 3 minutes. Divide this mixture between the ramekin dishes and smooth it out to cover the brown meat completely.

Wipe the saucepan and melt the remaining butter. Strain through a single thickness of absorbent kitchen paper, to remove the salt and any moisture in the fat. Pour this clarified butter over the crabmeat ramekins. Chill for up to 48 hours.

Serve with fingers of freshly made toast and lemon wedges. SERVES 4.

AVOCADO AND ORANGE FANS

3 avocados   1 tablespoon cooking oil
2 large oranges $\frac{1}{2}$ teaspoon caster sugar
shredded lettuce to garnish   salt and pepper
1 tablespoon lemon juice

CUT the avocados into halves and remove the stones.
Carefully peel off the skin. With a sharp knife, slice
lengthways through each avocado half, making cuts about
1 cm/$\frac{1}{2}$ in apart.

Grate the rind from 1 orange and reserve. Peel the
remaining oranges and remove all the pith from both
oranges with a sharp knife. Holding each orange over a
bowl to catch the juice, cut out the segments between the
membranes and set aside. Reserve the juice.

Place the avocado halves on plates and gently open out
the slices to make a fan. Place an orange segment between
each avocado slice. Decorate the plates with a little shredded lettuce.

Mix 1 teaspoon of the reserved orange rind into the
orange juice. Add the lemon juice, oil, sugar and salt and
pepper to taste. Spoon this dressing over the avocados.
Serve within 30 minutes. SERVES 6.

PLAICE AND PRAWN PIE

8 plaice fillets
100 g/4 oz peeled, cooked
   prawns
1 (298-g/10½-oz) can con-
   densed mushroom soup

1 (212-g/7½-oz) packet frozen
   puff pastry, thawed
milk or beaten egg to glaze

CUT the plaice fillets in half lengthways. Remove the skin
and roll up the fillets. Place in a 1.15-litre/2-pint pie dish.
Sprinkle with the prawns and spoon over the condensed
mushroom soup.

Roll out the pastry and use it to cover the pie. Brush with
milk or beaten egg and make a small hole in the centre.
Decorate with pastry trimmings, if wished. Bake in a hot
oven (220 C, 425 F, gas 7) for 10 minutes. Reduce heat to
moderately hot (190 C, 375 F, gas 5) and cook for a further
30 minutes until golden brown. Serve with new potatoes
and peas. SERVES 4.

COD STEAKS WITH CAMEMBERT

4 frozen cod steaks
1 tablespoon lemon juice
2 tablespoons plain flour,
     seasoned with salt and
     pepper
4 rashers rindless streaky
     bacon

25 g/1 oz butter
1 red pepper
75 g/3 oz Camembert cheese
1 tablespoon grated
     Parmesan cheese

SPRINKLE the cod steaks with the lemon juice and coat them in the seasoned flour. Cut the bacon into small pieces. Melt 15 g/½ oz butter in a frying pan and fry the bacon until crisp. Lift the bacon out with a slotted spoon and set aside. Reserve the fat.

Fry the cod steaks for 3 minutes on each side in the reserved fat. Lift them out and arrange in a shallow, ovenproof dish. Sprinkle the bacon over the fish. Cut the red pepper in half, deseed and slice finely. Scatter the sliced pepper over the fish. Cut the Camembert into small dice and arrange these over the red pepper. Sprinkle with the Parmesan and dot with a little butter. Bake in a moderately hot oven (190 C, 375 F, gas 5) for 20 to 25 minutes.

Serve with a salad or green beans and boiled new potatoes. SERVES 4.

THREE-PEPPER CHICKEN WITH TURNIPS

1 (1.5-kg/3½-lb) roasting
  chicken
50 g/2 oz butter or
  margarine
1 teaspoon cayenne
2 teaspoons paprika
1 teaspoon ground black
  pepper

1 teaspoon salt
1 small onion
6 small turnips
1 tablespoon flour
300 ml/½ pint chicken or
  giblet stock

PLACE the chicken in a roasting tin. Cream the butter or
margarine with the cayenne, paprika, black pepper and
salt. Place one-third of the mixture inside the chicken, with
the onion. Spread the remaining mixture over the skin.
Peel the turnips and arrange them around the chicken.
Cook in a moderately hot oven (200C, 400F, gas 6) for 1¼
hours, basting occasionally.

Lift the chicken on to a warm serving dish and surround
with the turnips. Pour off the excess fat from the roasting
tin. Stir the flour into the pan juices, gradually blend in the
stock and cook over a moderate heat until the gravy
thickens, then boil for 2 minutes.

Serve the chicken and turnips with the gravy, creamed
potatoes and a green vegetable. SERVES 6.

CHICKEN IN SPINACH PANCAKES

Pancakes
100 g/4 oz plain flour
2 eggs
2 teaspoons oil
150 ml/¼ pint milk
3 tablespoons water
225 g/8 oz fresh spinach,
   finely chopped
oil for frying
Filling
225 g/8 oz cooked chicken

25 g/1 oz butter or
   margarine
25 g/1 oz plain flour
300 ml/½ pint chicken stock
2 tablespoons single cream
salt and pepper
Topping
1 (425-g/15-oz) can tomatoes
50 g/2 oz Cheddar cheese,
   grated

PUT the flour in a bowl and add the eggs, oil and milk. Mix until smooth. Add the water and stir in the spinach.

Heat a little oil in a small frying or pancake pan. Pour off any excess oil to leave pan lightly greased. Pour in about 2 tablespoons of batter and quickly swirl the batter round the pan to coat. Cook over a moderate heat until brown underneath, toss or turn the pancake and continue cooking until the pancake is brown on both sides. Turn on to a plate. Cook the remaining batter in the same way to make about eight pancakes.

To make the filling, cut up the chicken. Heat the butter or margarine in a small saucepan, stir in the flour and cook for 2 minutes. Remove from the heat and stir in the stock. Return the pan to the heat and bring to the boil stirring constantly. Cook for 2 minutes. Remove from the heat and stir in the cream, chicken and seasoning.

Divide the chicken filling between the pancakes and roll up each pancake. Place the pancake rolls in a shallow, ovenproof dish. Pour over the canned tomatoes and sprinkle with the cheese. Cook in a moderately hot oven (200C, 400F, gas 6) for 25 minutes. Serve hot with a salad. SERVES 4.

TURKEY AND HAM PIE

450 g/1 lb cooked turkey	300 ml/½ pint boiling water
100 g/4 oz sliced ham	150 ml/¼ pint milk
2 hard-boiled eggs	3 cardamom seeds, crushed
50 g/2 oz butter or	salt and pepper
margarine	1 tablespoon chopped
1 onion, chopped	parsley
1 teaspoon curry powder	1 quantity Shortcrust Pastry
50 g/2 oz plain flour	(page 126)
1 chicken stock cube	beaten egg to glaze

CUT the turkey into bite-sized pieces. Cut the ham into 1-cm/½-in strips. Roughly chop the eggs. Put the turkey, ham and eggs into a 1.15-litre/2-pint pie dish.

Melt the butter or margarine in a saucepan, add the onion and curry powder and cook gently until the onion is soft. Add the flour and cook for 2 minutes. Dissolve the stock cube in the boiling water.

Remove the saucepan from the heat and blend in the stock and the milk, then add the cardamom seeds. Return the pan to the heat, bring to the boil and simmer for 3 minutes. Pour this sauce over the turkey mixture in the pie dish and mix well. Season with salt and pepper, then stir in the parsley. Allow to cool.

Roll out the Shortcrust Pastry and use it to cover the pie. Glaze the top with a little beaten egg and decorate with pastry trimmings, if wished. Cook in a moderately hot oven (200 C, 400 F, gas 6) until golden brown, about 30 minutes.

Serve hot with creamed potatoes and a green vegetable. SERVES 6 TO 8.

PORK WITH PRUNES AND SAGE

675 g/1½ lb pork fillet	1 tablespoon fresh sage,
25 g/1 oz plain flour	finely chopped
1 teaspoon paprika	1 (425-g/15-oz) can prunes
salt and pepper	in natural juice
40 g/1½ oz butter	4 tablespoons single cream

CUT the pork into 1-cm/½-in slices across the grain, trimming off any sinews. Mix the flour, paprika, salt and pepper and use to coat the pork slices.

Melt the butter in a large frying pan and fry the pork quickly until browned on all sides. Add the sage and fry for a further 2 minutes.

Drain the prunes, reserving the juice. Make the juice up to 150 ml/¼ pint with water. Add the juice to the pork. Bring to the boil and simmer for 15 minutes. Remove from the heat. Stone the prunes and add to the pork. Add the cream. Heat gently but do not boil.

Serve with new potatoes and mange-tout peas or a green salad. SERVES 4.

NAVARIN OF LAMB

8 best end cutlets of lamb	parsley sprig
25 g/1 oz plain flour	bay leaf
salt and pepper	225 g/8 oz young carrots
2 tablespoons oil	225 g/8 oz pickling onions
1 chicken stock cube	225 g/8 oz new potatoes
450 ml/¾ pint boiling water	2 small turnips
sprig of thyme	

TRIM any excess fat from the cutlets. Mix the flour with the salt and pepper and use to coat the cutlets. Heat the oil in a large frying pan and fry the cutlets until lightly browned on both sides. Place the cutlets in an ovenproof dish.

Stir any remaining flour into the fat in the pan. Dissolve the stock cube in the boiling water and blend this stock with the pan juices. Bring to the boil, then pour over the cutlets. Tie the thyme, parsley and bay leaf together and place in the dish with the cutlets. Cover and cook in a moderate oven (160 C, 325 F, gas 3) for 45 minutes.

Meanwhile, scrape the carrots and cut them into 1-cm/½-in slices. Peel the onions. Scrape the potatoes and cut any large ones in half. Peel and quarter the turnips. Add the vegetables to the lamb casserole, cover and continue cooking until the vegetables are tender, about another 45 minutes. Serve with French bread. SERVES 4.

HOLIDAY GAMMON

1 green gammon joint, about 2.75 kg/6 lb	1 tablespoon black treacle
225 g/8 oz cooking apples	cloves
	300 ml/½ pint dry cider

SOAK the gammon joint overnight in cold water. Weigh the joint and calculate the cooking time, allowing 30 minutes per 450 g/1 lb. Place the joint in a roasting tin and roast in a moderate oven (160 C, 325 F, gas 3) for half the calculated cooking time.

Meanwhile, peel, core and slice the apples. Place in a saucepan with 2 or 3 tablespoons water and cook until very soft and fairly dry. Do not let the apples stick. Stir in the black treacle.

Remove the gammon from the oven and peel off the skin. Stud the fat with cloves and spread the apple mixture over the joint. Return the joint to the oven and cook for the remaining cooking time, basting from time to time with the juices from the pan. Remove the joint to a warm serving dish and pour off the excess fat from the roasting tin. Pour the cider into the tin, mix with the meat juices and bring to the boil.

Serve the gammon with the cider sauce, a green vegetable and creamed potatoes. It is also delicious served cold with salad. SERVES 12 TO 15.

BEEF VALENTINE

225 g/8 oz rump steak	1 onion, sliced
1 tablespoon plain flour	150 ml/¼ pint beef stock
1 (50-g/2-oz) can anchovy fillets	3 tablespoons soured cream
25 g/1 oz butter	salt and pepper

CUT the steak into strips about 1 cm/½ in wide and 5 cm/ 2 in long. Toss the strips in the flour. Drain the anchovies and cut the fillets into pieces.

Heat the butter in a frying pan. Add the onion and fry for 3 minutes. Add the steak and anchovies and fry for 5 minutes, turning the pieces of steak so that they cook on all sides. Gradually stir in the stock and bring to the boil. Cook gently for 2 minutes. Stir in the cream and season to taste.

Serve on noodles with a green salad. SERVES 2.

STIR-FRIED CAULIFLOWER WITH BEAN SPROUTS

1 small cauliflower	50 g/2 oz blanched almonds
2 tablespoons oil	1 teaspoon cumin seeds
25 g/1 oz butter	1 teaspoon garam masala
225 g/8 oz fresh bean sprouts	salt and pepper

CUT the cauliflower into tiny florets about 2.5 cm/1 in long. Heat the oil and butter in a large frying pan or wok. Add the cauliflower, been sprouts, almonds, cumin and garam masala. Fry over a medium heat, stirring constantly, for about 5 minutes. Season with pepper and salt.

Serve hot with chops, steak or sausages. SERVES 4.

SPRING VEGETABLE LASAGNE

225 g/8 oz lasagne sheets	450 g/1 lb fresh spinach
50 g/2 oz butter or margarine	1 tablespoon water
50 g/2 oz plain flour	8 spring onions
600 ml/1 pint milk	225 g/8 oz cottage cheese
100 g/4 oz Cheddar cheese, grated	100 g/4 oz shelled peas
salt and pepper	1 clove garlic, crushed
	25 g/1 oz grated Parmesan cheese

COOK the lasagne in plenty of boiling, salted water, stirring occasionally, until just tender, about 10 to 15 minutes. Drain, return to the pan and cover with cold water to prevent the sheets from sticking together.

Meanwhile, melt the butter or margarine in a small saucepan, stir in the flour and cook for 1 minute. Gradually blend in the milk and bring to the boil, stirring constantly. Cook for 2 minutes. Stir in the Cheddar cheese and season well. Remove sauce from the heat and set aside.

Wash the spinach thoroughly and strip off the stalks. Chop the leaves. Place in a saucepan with the water and cook, stirring occasionally, for 2 or 3 minutes. Set aside and allow to cool.

Trim and chop the onions. Sieve the cottage cheese. Mix together the spinach, onions, cottage cheese, peas and garlic. Season well.

Grease a large, shallow, ovenproof dish. Place a layer of lasagne in the bottom. Cover this with a layer of the spinach mixture, then with a layer of sauce. Repeat layers until all the ingredients are used up, finishing with a layer of sauce. Sprinkle with Parmesan. Bake in the centre of a moderately hot oven (200 C, 400 F, gas 6) for about 30 minutes or until brown and bubbling. Serve hot with a salad. SERVES 6.

SAUCY CUCUMBER

1 large cucumber	25 g/1 oz plain flour
½ teaspoon salt	1 egg yolk
¼ teaspoon caster sugar	juice of ½ lemon
¼ teaspoon white pepper	¼ teaspoon ground nutmeg
600 ml/1 pint boiling water	finely chopped parsley to
1 chicken stock cube	garnish
25 g/1 oz butter	

PEEL the cucumber and cut it in half lengthways. Scoop out the seeds with a teaspoon, then cut each half into 1-cm/½-in slices. Place the slices in a saucepan with the salt, sugar, pepper, water and stock cube. Bring to the boil, cover and simmer gently until the cucumber is just tender, about 10 minutes. Drain, reserving the liquid.

Rinse the saucepan, then melt the butter, stir in the flour and cook for 2 minutes. Remove the pan from the heat and stir in the cucumber cooking liquid. Return to the heat and bring to the boil, stirring constantly. Cook for 2 minutes. Remove the pan from the heat.

Mix the egg yolk and lemon juice together. Whisk the yolk mixture into the sauce with the nutmeg. Return the cucumber pieces to the pan and reheat gently, without boiling. Turn into a warmed serving dish and sprinkle with the parsley. Serve with fish, poultry or white meat. SERVES 4.

HOT POTATO SALAD

675 g / 1½ lb new potatoes
4 rashers streaky bacon
1 onion, finely chopped
2 tablespoons white wine
   vinegar

2 tablespoons finely chopped
   parsley

WASH the potatoes and then cook them in their skins in boiling, salted water until just tender. Drain. Remove and discard the rind and bone from the bacon. Cut the rashers into small pieces and place them in a frying pan. Dry fry until crisp. Lift out the bacon pieces and reserve the fat.

Cut the hot potatoes into halves, if large, and place in a serving bowl. Add the onion and crisp bacon. Add the vinegar to the bacon fat and gently re-heat. (Be careful – the fat may froth.) Pour the vinegar mixture over the potatoes, add the parsley and mix lightly. Serve hot, with cold meats or poultry. SERVES 4.

WHOLEFOOD SALAD

100 g/4 oz green lentils	1 tablespoon chopped
100 g/4 oz long-grain	parsley
brown rice	*Dressing*
2 medium carrots	8 tablespoons sunflower oil
1 small onion	3 tablespoons cider vinegar
100 g/4 oz white cabbage	2 teaspoons clear honey
50 g/2 oz currants	salt and pepper
50 g/2 oz sunflower seeds	pinch of dry mustard

SOAK the lentils in cold water for 3 or 4 hours, or overnight. Drain. Cook the rice and the lentils in boiling, salted water until tender, about 30 minutes.

Meanwhile, peel and coarsely grate the carrots and onion and grate the cabbage. Drain the rice and lentils, rinse with cold water and drain again thoroughly. Mix the cooked rice and lentils with the carrot, onion, cabbage, currants, sunflower seeds and parsley in a salad bowl.

Put all the dressing ingredients in a small jar with a tight-fitting lid and shake well to mix. Pour the dressing over the salad and mix to combine. Serve the salad on its own as a light lunch or with cold roast chicken for a more substantial meal. SERVES 6.

Coeur à la Crème

2 egg whites	*To serve*
75 g/3 oz caster sugar	fresh or thawed frozen rasp-
300 ml/½ pint double cream	berries, strawberries or
300 ml/½ pint natural yogurt	blackberries

WHISK the egg whites until they are stiff but not dry. Gradually whisk in the sugar. Whip the cream until it holds its shape. Fold the yogurt into the cream and then fold the egg whites into the cream and yogurt.

Line six heart-shaped coeur-à-la-crème moulds or a large sieve with greaseproof paper. Spoon the cream mixture into the moulds or sieve. Place the moulds on a plate covered with absorbent kitchen paper or place the sieve over a bowl. Chill in the refrigerator overnight.

Turn out the moulds on to small plates or the sieve on to a large plate. Spoon the berries around the coeur à la crème just before serving. SERVES 6.

RHUBARB AND ORANGE SPONGE PUDDING

350 g/12 oz rhubarb
150 g/5 oz caster sugar
100 g/4 oz soft margarine
50 g/2 oz plain flour
2 eggs, separated

grated rind and juice of 1
  large orange
150 ml/¼ pint milk
single cream to serve

WASH the rhubarb and cut it into 1-cm/½-in lengths. Place in a 1.15-litre/2-pint ovenproof dish. Sprinkle with 25 g/1 oz sugar.

Cream the remaining sugar with the margarine. Stir in the flour, egg yolks, orange rind and juice and mix well. Gradually blend in the milk. Whisk the egg whites until stiff but not dry. Fold into the orange mixture and then pour over the rhubarb. Bake in a moderate oven (160 C, 325 F, gas 3) for 45 minutes, until golden brown. The pudding separates to give a fluffy sponge topping over an orange and rhubarb sauce. Serve warm with single cream. SERVES 6.

Variation
Apple and Lemon Sponge Pudding: Substitute thinly sliced cooking apples for the rhubarb, and lemon rind and juice for the orange. This variation is also delicious if half apples and half blackberries are used.

TUSCANY GRAPES

100 g/4 oz green grapes	4 tablespoons medium sweet
4 egg yolks	sherry
50 g/2 oz caster sugar	

HALVE the grapes and remove the pips. Divide them between 4 tall dessert glasses.

Place the egg yolks, sugar and sherry in a large basin over a pan of gently boiling water and whisk with an electric or rotary whisk until the yolks are very thick and frothy, about 7 minutes. Spoon this mixture over the grapes. Serve warm. SERVES 4.

GOOSEBERRY AND CHOCOLATE TART

1 quantity Shortcrust Pastry (page 126)	2 tablespoons cocoa
	50 g/2 oz caster sugar
225 g/8 oz gooseberries	1 egg
50 g/2 oz fresh breadcrumbs	single cream to serve
300 ml/½ pint milk	

LINE a 20-cm/8-in flan ring or flan dish with Shortcrust Pastry. Top and tail the gooseberries and place in the flan.

Put the breadcrumbs in a bowl. Heat the milk, cocoa and sugar together gently, then pour on to the breadcrumbs. Beat in the egg. Pour the mixture over the gooseberries. Cook in a moderately hot oven (190 C, 375 F, gas 5) for about 35 minutes. Serve warm with cream. SERVES 6.

APPLE CRÊPES BRÛLÉES

Crêpes
2 eggs
100 g/4 oz plain flour
25 g/1 oz butter, melted
175 ml/6 fl oz milk
oil for frying
Filling
4 medium eating apples

1 teaspoon ground
   cinnamon
2 tablespoons water
1 tablespoon caster sugar
Topping
300 ml/½ pint double cream
50 g/2 oz soft brown sugar

PLACE the eggs, flour and butter in a bowl. Gradually blend in the milk to make a smooth batter. Heat a little oil in a small frying or pancake pan. Pour off any excess oil to leave pan lightly greased. Pour in about 2 tablespoons of the batter and quickly swirl the batter round the pan to coat. Cook over a moderate heat until brown underneath, then toss or turn the crêpe with a palette knife and brown the other side. Turn on to a plate. Cook the remaining batter in the same way to make about ten crêpes, stacking them on top of each other.

To make the filling: peel, core and slice the apples. Place in a saucepan with the cinnamon, water and sugar. Cover and cook over a low heat for 5 minutes, until the water is absorbed but the apple slices are still slightly firm. Divide the apple mixture between the crêpes, roll up each crêpe and place in a shallow, ovenproof dish. Do not pile them up more than two deep. Spoon the cream over the pancakes to cover. Chill.

Just before serving, prepare a hot grill. Sprinkle the brown sugar over the cream and place the dish under the grill until the sugar is brown and bubbling. Serve at once. SERVES 4.

HOT CROSS BUNS

675 g/1½ lb strong plain flour	50 g/2 oz cut mixed peel
pinch of salt	1 egg, beaten
2 teaspoons mixed spice	*Crosses*
50 g/2 oz butter	75 g/3 oz plain flour
15 g/½ oz fresh yeast *or*	4 tablespoons water
1 sachet easy-blend yeast	*Glaze*
300 ml/½ pint warm water	2 tablespoons caster sugar
25 g/1 oz caster sugar	1 tablespoon milk
50 g/2 oz currants	

SIFT the flour, salt and mixed spice into a large bowl. Rub in the butter. If using fresh yeast, blend it with a little of the water to a smooth cream, then gradually blend in the remaining water. If using easy-blend yeast, stir it straight into the flour and spice mixture.

Make a well in the flour mixture and pour in the yeast liquid, or the warm water if easy-blend yeast is used. Add the sugar, currants, peel and egg. Mix well to combine. Turn out on to a floured surface and knead the dough until it is elastic. Replace in the bowl, cover with a lightly oiled polythene sheet and leave in a warm place to rise for about 1 hour, or until doubled in bulk.

Turn out and knead lightly. Cut into 16 equal pieces. Shape each piece into a smooth ball and flatten between your hands. Place the buns on greased baking trays, well apart to allow room for rising. Cover with polythene and leave the buns to rise in a warm place for about 30 minutes.

Meanwhile, mix the flour and water for the crosses to a thick paste. Place the mixture in a piping bag fitted with a 5-mm/¼-in plain tube. When the buns have risen, pipe crosses on each with the flour paste. Bake the buns in a hot oven (220 C, 425 F, gas 7) for 15 to 20 minutes, until brown. The buns should sound hollow when tapped on the base.

To make the glaze: dissolve the sugar in the milk and bring to the boil. Remove from the heat. Place the cooked buns on a wire rack, brush immediately with the glaze and leave to cool slightly. Serve warm. MAKES 16.

TEA BREAD

225 g/8 oz sultanas
50 g/2 oz cut mixed peel
100 g/4 oz soft light brown sugar

150 ml/$\frac{1}{4}$ pint warm tea
1 egg
225 g/8 oz self-raising flour

PLACE the sultanas, peel and sugar in a bowl. Add the tea and leave to soak for at least 1 hour. Grease a 450-g/1-lb loaf tin.

Stir the egg into the fruit mixture and beat well. Sift the flour on to the fruit and mix well. Turn the mixture into the tin. Bake in a moderate oven (160 C, 325 F, gas 3) for about $1\frac{1}{2}$ hours. When cooked, the loaf should spring back when pressed with a finger. Leave it to cool in the tin for 10 minutes, then turn it out and leave to cool completely on a wire rack. This loaf improves if kept in an airtight tin for a day or two. Serve sliced and buttered. MAKES 1 LOAF.

MAGPIE SQUARES

175 g/6 oz self-raising flour
175 g/6 oz desiccated
   coconut
100 g/4 oz soft brown sugar
175 g/6 oz butter or
   margarine, melted
Filling
350 g/12 oz icing sugar

50 g/2 oz butter or
   margarine, melted
3 tablespoons milk
1 teaspoon peppermint
   essence
Topping
100 g/4 oz cooking chocolate

MIX the flour, coconut and sugar together. Mix in the melted butter or margarine. Press the mixture into a greased 27 × 18 × 4-cm/10½ × 7 × 1½-in tin. Bake in a moderate oven (180C, 350F, gas 4) for 20 minutes.

Meanwhile, mix all the filling ingredients together. Spread the filling over the hot coconut base and leave to cool in the tin.

Melt the chocolate in a flameproof bowl over a pan of simmering water. Spread the melted chocolate carefully over the peppermint filling. Leave to set. When set, cut into 24 squares. MAKES 24.

ELDERFLOWER JELLY

600 ml/1 pint loosely packed
   elderflowers
1.5 kg/3 lb cooking apples
900 ml/1½ pints water

3 tablespoons white wine
   vinegar
granulated or preserving
   sugar (see method)

WASH the elderflowers and remove as much stalk as possible. Wash and cut up the apples. Place the apples and elderflowers in a preserving pan with the water and vinegar. Bring to the boil and simmer until the apples are soft and pulpy. Pour into a jelly bag and leave to drip overnight.

Next day, measure the juice into a clean preserving pan and add 450 g/1 lb sugar for each 600 ml/1 pint juice. Bring to the boil slowly, stirring until the sugar has dissolved. Boil rapidly until the jelly begins to set, then skim and remove from the heat. Allow to cool, then pot, cover with waxed paper discs and label.

This jelly is delicious with hot or cold chicken, game, pork or lamb. MAKES ABOUT 1.5 KG/3 LB.

RHUBARB AND GINGER JAM

1 kg/2 lb young, tender rhubarb
1 kg/2 lb preserving sugar with pectin
5-cm/2-in piece fresh root ginger

grated rind of 1 lemon
juice of 2 lemons
50 g/2 oz crystallised ginger, chopped (optional)

CUT the rhubarb into 2.5-cm/1-in lengths, discarding the leaves and the root ends. Place the rhubarb and sugar in a preserving pan.

Peel the root ginger and grate coarsely into the preserving pan. Add the lemon rind and juice. Place the pan over a low heat and stir occasionally until the juice begins to run from the rhubarb and the sugar has dissolved. Bring to a full, rolling boil and boil for 4 minutes. Remove from the heat and stir in the chopped crystallised ginger (if used). Pot, cover and label the jam. MAKES ABOUT 2.5 KG/5 LB.

MINTED ICED TEA

4 generous teaspoons tea
 leaves or 4 tea bags
4 sprigs mint
900 ml/1½ pints boiling water
ice cubes

caster sugar
Garnish
lemon slices
mint sprigs

PLACE the tea in a teapot with the mint. Pour on the boiling water and leave to infuse for 3 minutes. Fill four tall, heatproof glasses with ice cubes, pour on the tea and sweeten with sugar to taste. Garnish each glass with a slice of lemon and a sprig of mint. SERVES 4.

CHOCOLATE MALTED MILKSHAKE

2 tablespoons cocoa
50 g/2 oz caster sugar
3 tablespoons boiling water
2 tablespoons malted milk
 powder

1 teaspoon vanilla essence
450 ml/¾ pint chilled milk
2 scoops vanilla or chocolate
 icecream

MIX the cocoa and sugar together, then blend in the boiling water. Blend in a liquidiser with the malted milk powder, vanilla essence and milk. Add the icecream and blend again until frothy. Pour into glasses and serve with straws. SERVES 2.

Variations
Coffee Malted: Omit the cocoa and vanilla essence. Mix 2 tablespoons of instant coffee with the sugar and water, then proceed as above.
Banana Malted: Omit the cocoa, boiling water and vanilla essence. Mash 1 large banana with the sugar, then proceed as above.

SUMMER

THERE is an abundance of fresh produce during the summer months, the vegetables are young and tender and need little or no cooking which saves many hours of preparation in the kitchen. Meals should be light and tasty and during hot spells salads and cold dishes are much more appetising than hot meals. Chilled starters like Greek Cucumber Soup or Smoked Trout Mousse are quick to make and Chicken Galantine or Spiced Beef are economical joints which can be served cold with salads. Black Cherry Icecream or Coffee Sorbet make refreshing desserts.

Fish and chicken are good barbecue foods and you'll find two unusual ideas in this chapter. A jug of Lemonade in the refrigerator will be a popular refreshment and don't forget to stock up the store cupboard with home-made preserves such as Raspberry and Redcurrant Jam and Tomato and Onion Chutney.

GREEK CUCUMBER SOUP

1 large cucumber	2 tablespoons finely chopped
about 1 tablespoon salt	mint
2 cloves garlic, crushed	white pepper
450 ml/¾ pint natural yogurt	mint sprigs for garnish
150 ml/¼ pint single cream	
2 tablespoons white wine	
vinegar	

PEEL the cucumber, cut it into very small dice and put these in a colander or large sieve. Sprinkle with the salt. Leave to drain over a bowl for about 1 hour, then rinse with cold water and dry thoroughly in a clean tea-towel. Place the cucumber in a bowl and add the garlic, yogurt, cream, vinegar and chopped mint. Mix together very well. Season with pepper and more salt, if necessary. Chill for about 2 hours. Serve garnished with mint sprigs. SERVES 4.

CHILLED APRICOT SOUP

2 (425-g/15-oz) cans apricot	150 ml/¼ pint dry white wine
halves in natural juice	150 ml/¼ pint single cream
1 teaspoon ground	25 g/1 oz flaked almonds,
cinnamon	toasted

THIS soup makes a very refreshing summer starter.

Purée the apricots with their juice in a liquidiser. Add the cinnamon and wine and blend until smooth. Chill for 1 or 2 hours.

To serve, spoon the soup into small glass or china bowls, swirl single cream on each serving and sprinkle with flaked almonds. SERVES 6.

PASTA WITH BASIL AND ALMONDS

50 g/2 oz blanched almonds
225 g/8 oz tagliatelle
1 clove garlic, crushed
3 tablespoons chopped fresh
   basil

150 ml/¼ pint single cream
25 g/1 oz butter
salt and pepper

CUT the almonds into thin slivers and cook under a moderate grill until golden brown.

Cook the tagliatelle in plenty of boiling, salted water until just tender, about 10 minutes. Drain. Return the pasta to the pan and stir in the garlic, basil, cream, butter and seasoning. (Freshly ground black pepper is best for this dish.) Stir over a low heat for 2 or 3 minutes. Serve sprinkled with the slivered almonds. SERVES 4.

Variation
Pasta with Bacon and Cashew Nuts: Omit basil and almonds. Fry 100 g/4 oz finely chopped bacon until crisp and stir into pasta with 1 tablespoon chopped parsley and sprinkle with 50 g/2 oz chopped browned cashew nuts.

JELLIED GAZPACHO

225 g/8 oz ripe tomatoes	1 tablespoon olive oil
1 small onion, chopped	1 tablespoon white wine
¼ cucumber, chopped	vinegar
1 small green pepper	½ teaspoon caster sugar
1 clove garlic, crushed	salt and pepper
300 ml/½ pint tomato juice	15 g/½ oz powdered gelatine
2 tablespoons tomato purée	2 tablespoons hot water

COVER the tomatoes with boiling water, leave for 30 seconds, then drain them and slip off the skins. Roughly chop the tomatoes and place the pieces in a liquidiser. Add the onion and cucumber. Chop the pepper, discarding the core and seeds, and add the pieces to the other vegetables, with the garlic. Blend these ingredients until smooth. Add the tomato juice, tomato purée, oil, vinegar and sugar and season well.

Place the gelatine and hot water in a small heatproof bowl over a pan of gently simmering water, then stir until the gelatine has dissolved. With the liquidiser running, gradually add the gelatine.

Pour the gazpacho into six small glass dishes and leave in the refrigerator to set. Serve well chilled with fingers of fried bread. SERVES 6.

SMOKED TROUT MOUSSE

2 smoked trout	½ teaspoon salt
150 ml/¼ pint single cream	*Garnish*
2 tablespoons lemon juice	6 lemon slices
100 g/4 oz cottage cheese	chopped parsley
¼ teaspoon cayenne	

REMOVE the skin and bones from the trout. Flake the fish and place in a liquidiser or food processor. Add the cream, lemon juice, cottage cheese, cayenne and salt. Blend until smooth. Divide the mixture between six small ramekin dishes. Smooth the tops and chill thoroughly.

Before serving, top each mousse with a slice of lemon and sprinkle with chopped parsley. Serve with Melba Toast (see page 125). SERVES 6.

BARBECUED TROUT

4 fresh trout	4 sprigs fresh fennel or dill
oil	lemon juice

ASK your fishmonger to clean the trout. Brush the fish well with oil, tuck a sprig of fennel or dill into the body cavity and place the fish on the barbecue in wire fish-cookers or directly on to the barbecue grill. Cook for 10 minutes on each side, or until the fish flakes easily.

Squeeze a little lemon juice over each fish and serve hot with new potatoes and a green salad. SERVES 4.

SUMMER SALMON STEAKS

butter for greasing
4 salmon steaks, about
    2.5 cm/1 in thick
4 teaspoons lemon juice
salt and pepper
4 sprigs fresh fennel or dill

6 tablespoons thick
    mayonnaise
2 teaspoons gelatine
2 tablespoons hot water
lemon slices and parsley
    sprigs to garnish

BUTTER four squares of aluminium foil large enough to enclose the salmon steaks. Place one steak on each piece of foil and sprinkle each one with 1 teaspoon lemon juice, salt and pepper. Top with a sprig of fennel or dill.

Wrap the foil around the steaks and place them in a roasting tin. Add enough water to cover the base of the tin and cook the salmon in a moderately hot oven (190C, 375 F, gas 5) for 20 to 25 minutes, or until the salmon flakes when tested with the point of a knife. Leave to cool in the foil.

Strain the liquid from the foil packets into a measuring jug and make up to 150 ml/$\frac{1}{4}$ pint with water. Arrange the salmon steaks on a dish and remove the fennel or dill. Carefully peel off the skin and ease out the central bone from each steak.

Stir the mayonnaise into the reserved fish liquid. Stir the gelatine into the hot water in a small heatproof basin, then place the basin over a pan of gently simmering water and stir until the gelatine has dissolved. Add the gelatine to the mayonnaise mixture, then spoon mayonnaise over the salmon steaks to cover.

To serve, decorate with lemon slices and parsley. SERVES 4.

BARBECUED CHICKEN SATAY
WITH PEANUT SAUCE

450 g/1 lb boned chicken
   breast meat
1 medium onion, finely
   chopped
1 small green pepper,
   deseeded and finely
   chopped
3 tablespoons lemon juice
3 tablespoons soy sauce
½ teaspoon garlic salt
1 tablespoon oil
1 teaspoon caster
   sugar

Peanut Sauce
4 tablespoons desiccated
   coconut
300 ml/½ pint boiling water
1 tablespoon oil
1 small onion, chopped
1 clove garlic, crushed
juice of ½ lemon
4 tablespoons peanut butter
½ teaspoon chilli powder
1 teaspoon soft brown sugar
1 teaspoon salt
1 bay leaf

CUT the chicken into 2.5-cm/1-in dice. Put the onion and
green pepper in a bowl and add the lemon juice, soy sauce,
garlic salt, oil and caster sugar. Mix well. Fold in the diced
chicken and leave to marinate for 2 hours.

Meanwhile, make the peanut sauce: put the coconut in a
measuring jug and pour on the water. Leave for 15
minutes, then strain through a sieve, reserving the liquor
and pressing to extract all the liquid from the coconut.

Heat the oil in a small saucepan, then add the onion and
garlic and cook over a moderate heat until the onion is soft.
Stir in the coconut liquor, lemon juice, peanut butter, chilli
powder, sugar, salt and bay leaf. Bring to the boil, stirring
constantly, then cover and simmer for 10 minutes. Remove
the bay leaf before serving.

Thread the chicken on to six metal skewers. Cook over a
barbecue or under a hot grill for 7 to 10 minutes, basting
occasionally with the marinade.

Serve the hot chicken with the peanut sauce. Sliced or
diced cucumber makes an excellent accompaniment for
this dish. SERVES 6.

CHICKEN GALANTINE

1 chicken, about 1.5 kg/3½ lb
salt and pepper
Stuffing
1 medium onion, finely
  chopped
225 g/8 oz pork sausagemeat
100 g/4 oz ham, chopped
1 tablespoon chopped fresh
  tarragon or parsley

juice and grated rind of 1
  lemon
12 black olives
To finish
8 tablespoons mayonnaise
cucumber and tomato slices
  to garnish

PLACE the chicken on a board, breast side down. Cut off
the wing tips and the legs at the first joint. Using a small,
sharp knife, make a cut down the centre of the back.
Carefully scrape the skin and flesh away from the rib cage.
When you reach the wing and thigh joints, cut through the
joint nearest to the body and continue cutting the flesh
away from the rib cage, until it is held only by the tip of the
breast bone. Carefully cut away the flesh from the breast
bone, being careful not to puncture the skin. Remove the
rib cage. Scrape the flesh away from the wing bones,
turning the wings inside out as the bone is exposed. Repeat
with the leg bones, also turning these inside out.

Put the chicken bones in a saucepan, cover with water
and season well. Bring to the boil and simmer for 1½ hours.

Meanwhile, mix the onion, sausagemeat, ham, tarragon
or parsley and lemon rind and juice. Discard the stones
from the olives, chop the flesh and add to the stuffing. Mix
well and season.

Lay the boned chicken on a board, skin side down.
Arrange the stuffing down the centre. Draw the long sides
of chicken together and sew with fine string. Wrap the
chicken in muslin and tie securely.

Place the chicken in a saucepan and pour in the stock
from the chicken bones. Cover and simmer for 1½ hours.

Lift out the chicken and reserve the stock. Place the chicken between two plates, then place a weight on top to press. Allow to cool. When cold, remove the muslin and string.

Reduce the chicken stock by boiling rapidly for 5 minutes. Blend 4 tablespoons of the reduced stock with the mayonnaise and spoon this over the galantine to coat. The chicken stock will set the mayonnaise. Garnish with the cucumber and tomato. SERVES 6.

Variations
Chicken Galantine with Veal: Substitute 225 g/8 oz finely minced veal and 50 g/2 oz fresh breadcrumbs for the sausagemeat. Omit olives but add 50 g/2 oz chopped blanched almonds to stuffing. Cook as above.
Chicken Galantine with Egg: Hard boil 3 eggs and remove shells. Spread stuffing over boned chicken. Place eggs in a line down centre then carefully wrap chicken and stuffing over eggs and sew up. Cook as above.
Chicken Galantine with Salami: Spread stuffing over chicken as in previous variation. Arrange slices of salami over stuffing and a row of gherkins down the centre. Wrap chicken, stuffing and salami around gherkins and sew up. Cook as above.

DUCK WITH GOOSEBERRY SAUCE

6 duck portions	1 teaspoon chopped fresh
oil	thyme or ¼ teaspoon dried
salt and pepper	thyme
Gooseberry Sauce	*Gravy*
225 g/8 oz gooseberries	1 tablespoon plain flour
5 tablespoons water	1 chicken stock cube
2 tablespoons caster sugar	300 ml/½ pint boiling water
25 g/1 oz butter	few drops gravy browning

PUT the duck portions on a rack in a roasting tin. Brush with oil and sprinkle with salt and pepper. Roast in a moderately hot oven (190 C, 375 F, gas 5) for 1¼ hours, or until the juices run clear when the skin is pierced.

Meanwhile, make the sauce. Top and tail the gooseberries and place in a saucepan with the water and sugar. Cook gently until the gooseberries are soft, then stir in the butter and thyme.

When the duck portions are cooked, arrange them on a warm serving dish. Pour off the fat from the roasting tin, then stir the flour into the juices in the tin and cook over a moderate heat for 2 minutes. Dissolve the stock cube in the boiling water and stir into the tin, then bring to the boil and cook for 2 minutes. Colour with the gravy browning.

Serve the duck with gravy, gooseberry sauce, new potatoes and peas. SERVES 6.

VEAL WITH TUNA

4 veal escalopes	1 tablespoon lemon juice
1 (50-g/2-oz) can anchovy fillets	6 tablespoons thick mayonnaise
25 g/1 oz butter	salt and pepper
150 ml/¼ pint chicken stock	*To serve*
1 (99-g/3½-oz) can tuna	lettuce
1 teaspoon grated lemon rind	1 tablespoon capers

FLATTEN the veal escalopes by beating with a rolling pin. Place an anchovy fillet at the short end of each escalope, then roll up the escalope round the anchovy and secure with a wooden cocktail stick. Repeat with the remaining escalopes.

Melt the butter in a saucepan large enough to hold all the escalopes in a single layer. Fry the escalopes until golden on all sides. Pour on the stock. Cover and simmer until the veal is tender, about 20 minutes. Leave to cool in the saucepan.

Put the remaining anchovy fillets, drained tuna and lemon rind and juice in a food processor or liquidiser and blend until the mixture is puréed. Add the mayonnaise and seasoning and blend again until well mixed.

Shred the lettuce and arrange on a serving dish. Remove the cocktail sticks from the veal rolls and arrange the veal on the lettuce. Spoon the mayonnaise mixture over the veal and sprinkle the capers over the top. SERVES 4.

BARBECUED BRIE-FILLED BURGERS

675 g/1½ lb lean minced beef
1 large potato, grated
1 teaspoon dry mustard
1 tablespoon chopped fresh
　mixed herbs or 1 teaspoon
　dried mixed herbs

salt and pepper
75 g/3 oz ripe Brie cheese
oil
To serve
6 pitta breads
shredded lettuce

COMBINE the beef, potato, mustard, herbs and seasoning.
Divide the mixture into 12 equal-sized pieces. Cut the Brie
into six equal pieces. Flatten one piece of meat into a 7.5-
cm/3-in round on a floured surface. Place a piece of Brie in
the centre and flatten slightly. Cover with another round of
meat and press down firmly to seal. Repeat with the
remaining meat and cheese.

Brush the hamburgers with oil and cook on a hot
barbecue or under a hot grill for 3 to 5 minutes on each side.

Warm the pitta breads and open them out, then tuck a
little shredded lettuce and a hamburger in each. Serve at
once. SERVES 6.

BEEF AND VEGETABLE LOAF

1 large onion	salt and pepper
675 g/1½ lb minced beef	225 g/8 oz carrots
50 g/2 oz soft, brown breadcrumbs	225 g/8 oz potatoes
1 tablespoon chopped fresh herbs	225 g/8 oz courgettes
1 tablespoon French mustard	1 egg, beaten

PEEL and chop the onion and mix with the minced beef, breadcrumbs, herbs, mustard and seasoning. Spread the mixture out on a piece of greaseproof paper, to make a rectangle the length of a 1-kg/2-lb loaf tin and twice as wide.

Peel and grate the carrots and potatoes. Grate the courgettes. Mix the vegetables with the beaten egg and season well. Place this mixture down the centre of the meat and, using the paper to help, roll the meat around the vegetables.

Grease a 1-kg/2-lb loaf tin. Place the beef roll in the tin, removing the paper, and press down firmly. Cover the tin with aluminium foil and cook in a moderate oven (180C, 350F, gas 4) for 1 hour. Remove the foil and cook for a further 30 minutes.

Turn out the loaf and serve hot, cut into slices, with a green vegetable. Alternatively, leave the loaf to cool in the tin and serve cold, with salad. SERVES 6 TO 8.

SPICED BEEF

1 (1.5-kg/3-lb) joint topside or silverside of beef
12 cloves
2 medium onions, sliced
2 medium carrots, sliced
1 teaspoon ground allspice
1 teaspoon ground nutmeg
1 tablespoon black peppercorns

1 teaspoon salt
50 g/2 oz soft brown sugar
2 bay leaves
150 ml/¼ pint wine vinegar
300 ml/½ pint water
15 g/½ oz lard

WIPE the beef, stud it with the cloves and place in a bowl or deep dish, just large enough to hold it.

Combine the onions, carrots, allspice, nutmeg, peppercorns, salt, sugar, bay leaves, vinegar and water in a saucepan. Bring to the boil, then pour over the beef. Cover with cling film and refrigerate for 48 hours, turning the beef in the marinade every 12 hours.

Drain the meat, reserving the marinade. Heat the lard in a flameproof casserole dish, then add the beef and brown it quickly on all sides. Pour in the marinade. Cover and cook in a moderate oven (180 C, 350 F, gas 4) for 2 hours, basting the joint with the marinade occasionally. Remove from the oven and leave the beef to cool in the marinade. Serve thinly sliced with salad. SERVES 6 TO 8.

FRENCH BEANS MIMOSA

225 g/8 oz young French beans	1 hard-boiled egg
	15 g/½ oz butter

TOP and tail the beans, then cook them in boiling, salted water until they are just tender.

Meanwhile, shell the egg and very finely chop the white and sieve the yolk.

When the beans are cooked, drain well, toss in butter and arrange on a shallow dish. Sprinkle the egg yolk over the centre of the beans and the egg white around the outside. Serve hot. SERVES 4.

POTATO AND CUCUMBER SALAD

450 g/1 lb potatoes, cooked	pinch of salt
1 small cooked beetroot	pinch of pepper
3 spring onions	pinch of caster sugar
¼ teaspoon caraway seeds	2 teaspoons chopped fresh
150 ml/¼ pint soured cream	dill or ½ teaspoon dried
½ cucumber	dill
1 tablespoon oil	few sprigs dill to garnish
2 teaspoons lemon juice	(optional)

DICE the potatoes, peel and dice the beetroot and chop the onions. Place the vegetables in a salad bowl. Add the caraway seeds and soured cream and mix well.

Peel and thinly slice the cucumber, then arrange it over the potato mixture. Combine the oil, lemon juice, salt, pepper, sugar and dill in a small jar and shake well to mix. Pour this dressing over the cucumber. Decorate with dill sprigs, if available. SERVES 4.

MEDITERRANEAN SALAD

1 Webb's lettuce	*Dressing*
3 large tomatoes	1 clove garlic, crushed
½ cucumber	6 tablespoons olive oil
225 g/8 oz small French beans	2 tablespoons white wine
12 black or green olives	vinegar
1 teaspoon chopped fresh	salt and pepper
basil	pinch of caster sugar
1 tablespoon chopped parsley	pinch of dry mustard

TRIM, wash and drain the lettuce. Break it into chunky pieces and place in a salad bowl. Slice the tomatoes and cucumber and add to the bowl. Top and tail the beans, then cook in boiling, salted water for 5 minutes. Drain, rinse with cold water, drain again and add to the bowl. Add the olives and sprinkle with the herbs.

Shake all the dressing ingredients in a screw-topped jar. Pour over the salad and toss well. SERVES 4 TO 6.

SALAD STIR-FRY

¼ cucumber	1 tablespoon sesame seeds
1 small red pepper	salt and pepper
1 small green pepper	2 tablespoons white wine
2 tablespoons corn oil	vinegar
6 spring onions, sliced	
¼ head Chinese leaves,	
shredded	

CUT cucumber into thin sticks. Halve, deseed and slice peppers. Heat the oil in a wok or large frying pan. Stir-fry vegetables over a high heat for 5 minutes. Add sesame seeds and cook for a minute. Season generously and sprinkle with vinegar. Serve warm. SERVES 4 TO 6.

PEAS TARTARE

350 g/12 oz fresh shelled or
  frozen peas
1 hard-boiled egg
1 teaspoon finely chopped
  fresh mint
1 teaspoon finely chopped
  parsley

1 teaspoon finely chopped
  fresh tarragon
1 tablespoon capers
3 generous tablespoons
  mayonnaise
lettuce leaves to serve

COOK the peas in boiling, salted water until tender, about
12 minutes for fresh peas or 5 minutes for frozen peas.
Drain and rinse with cold water.

Shell and finely chop the egg. Mix the peas, egg, mint,
parsley, tarragon and capers into the mayonnaise and mix
lightly. Serve in a bowl lined with lettuce. SERVES 4.

RICE AND YOGURT MOULD

50 g/2 oz short-grain rice
600 ml/1 pint milk
75 g/3 oz caster sugar
15 g/½ oz powdered gelatine

2 tablespoons water
450 ml/¾ pint natural yogurt
450 g/1 lb strawberries

PUT the rice in a saucepan with the milk, bring to the boil,
then simmer very gently until the rice is tender, stirring
often to prevent the rice sticking. Remove from the heat
and add sugar. Sprinkle the gelatine over the water, stir
well, then add to the rice and stir until dissolved. Cool for
15 minutes, then stir in the yogurt.

Turn the rice mixture into a lightly oiled 1.15-litre/2-pint
ring mould. Tap the mould sharply to make sure that there
are no air bubbles in the rice. Allow to cool, then chill.

Turn out the rice mould on to a plate. Hull the strawberries and cut any very large ones in half. Arrange the
fruit in the centre of the rice ring and serve. SERVES 6.

ORANGE AND RASPBERRY CHEESECAKE

Base
175 g/6 oz digestive biscuits
75 g/3 oz butter
25 g/1 oz demerara sugar
Filling
450 g/1 lb cream cheese
75 g/3 oz caster sugar
grated rind and juice of
    1 large orange

2 eggs, beaten
150 ml/¼ pint single cream
225 g/8 oz raspberries
Topping
150 ml/¼ pint soured cream
2 teaspoons caster sugar

CRUSH the biscuits in a paper bag with a rolling pin. Melt the butter, stir in the crushed biscuits and demerara sugar. Press into the bottom of a greased 20-cm/8-in loose-bottomed cake tin.

Cream the cheese and sugar together. Stir in the grated orange rind and juice, and the beaten eggs. Fold in the cream, then carefully mix in the raspberries. Pour into tin and cook in the centre of a moderately hot oven (190 C, 375 F, gas 5) for 25 to 30 minutes until just set.

Meanwhile, make the topping. Mix the soured cream and sugar together. Pour over cheesecake and return to oven for 5 minutes. Leave to cool in the tin for about 1 hour. Then carefully ease the cheesecake out of the tin and slide off base. Chill before serving. SERVES 6 TO 8.

PEACHES AND CREAM PIE

1 quantity Shortcrust Pastry
(page 126)
4 fresh peaches
300 ml/½ pint single cream

75 g/3 oz caster sugar
2 eggs
2 tablespoons peach or
apricot jam

ROLL out the Shortcrust Pastry and use to line a 20-cm/8-in flan tin. Line the flan with greaseproof paper and fill with baking beans. Cook in a moderately hot oven (200 C, 400 F, gas 6) for 10 minutes. Remove the beans and the paper and return to the oven for 5 minutes, to cook the centre.

Cover the peaches with boiling water, leave for 30 seconds, then drain and peel. Cut the peaches into halves and remove the stones.

Whisk the cream, sugar and eggs together. Spread the jam in the base of the flan, arrange the peach halves on top, then pour over the cream mixture. Cook in a moderate oven (180 C, 350 F, gas 4) until set, about 30 minutes. Serve warm or cold. SERVES 6.

BLACK CHERRY ICECREAM

225 g/8 oz black cherries
3 tablespoons water
100 g/4 oz caster sugar
2 eggs, separated

450 ml/¾ pint whipping
  cream
1 teaspoon almond essence

STONE the cherries and put them in a saucepan with the water and 25 g/1 oz of the sugar. Bring to the boil, cover and simmer for 5 minutes.

Whisk the egg yolks with the remaining sugar until they are thick and light in colour. Bring the cream to the boil, then whisk it into the egg mixture with the almond essence. Allow to cool.

Whisk the egg whites until stiff, but not dry, fold into the cream mixture and pour into a shallow metal or plastic container. Freeze for about 1 hour, or until partially frozen.

Turn the icecream out into a bowl and whisk until smooth, then fold in cherries and their syrup. Return the mixture to the container and freeze until firm. SERVES 4 TO 6.

Variations

Strawberry Icecream: Omit the cherries, water and almond essence. Mash 225 g/8 oz strawberries with 25 g/1 oz sugar, then continue as above.

Chocolate Icecream: Omit the cherries and water and substitute vanilla essence for almond essence. Melt 100 g/4 oz plain chocolate in the cream, then continue as above.

COFFEE SORBET
WITH WHITE CHOCOLATE SAUCE

100 g/4 oz caster sugar	1 egg white
50 g/2 oz soft dark brown	*Sauce*
sugar	50 g/2 oz white chocolate
2 tablespoons instant coffee	5 tablespoons single cream
300 ml/½ pint water	

PUT the sugars, coffee and water in a saucepan and stir over a gentle heat until the sugars have dissolved. Then bring the mixture to the boil and boil gently for 3 minutes. Allow to cool, then pour the syrup into a shallow 1.15-litre/2-pint tin. Freeze until firm.

Whisk the egg white until very stiff but not dry. Turn the coffee mixture into a bowl and whisk until very pale in colour. Fold in the whisked egg white, then return to the freezer and freeze until firm.

To make the sauce: Break up the chocolate and place it in a saucepan with the cream. Stir over a low heat until the chocolate melts. Allow to cool.

Serve the sorbet in frosted glasses, with a little of the sauce spooned over the top. SERVES 4 TO 6.

MIDSUMMER GÂTEAU

Meringue
100 g/4 oz blanched
    almonds, toasted
4 egg whites
250 g/9 oz caster sugar
½ teaspoon almond essence
½ teaspoon vinegar

Filling
225 g/8 oz fresh apricots
4 egg yolks
1 tablespoon caster sugar
2 teaspoons cornflour
150 ml/¼ pint double cream

GREASE two 20-cm/8-in sandwich tins and line the bases
with Bakewell paper. Finely chop or grind the almonds.

Whisk the egg whites until very stiff but not dry.
Gradually fold in the sugar, almond essence and vinegar,
then the almonds. Divide the mixture between the two tins
and level the tops. Bake in the centre of a moderately hot
oven (190 C, 375 F, gas 5) for about 40 minutes, or until
lightly browned. Remove from the oven and leave to cool
in the tins. When cold, turn the meringue out on to a wire
rack and remove the paper.

While the meringue is cooling, make the filling. Halve
and finely chop the apricots. Place the egg yolks, sugar and
cornflour in a saucepan and mix well. Gradually blend in
the cream. Cook over a low heat, stirring constantly, until
the mixture thickens and holds its shape. Do not allow the
mixture to boil. Stir in the apricots and leave to cool,
stirring occasionally.

When both the filling and the meringue are quite cold,
place one meringue round on a plate, spread the filling on
top and cover it with the remaining round. Chill. SERVES
6 TO 8.

ROSEMARY FRUIT CAKE

175 g/6 oz butter or
margarine
175 g/6 oz soft light brown
sugar
3 eggs, beaten
225 g/8 oz plain flour

1 teaspoon baking powder
450 g/1 lb mixed dried fruit
1 tablespoon finely chopped
fresh young rosemary
leaves

GREASE a 20-cm/8-in deep, round cake tin and line with greased greaseproof paper.

Cream the fat and sugar together until light and fluffy, then gradually beat in the egg, alternately with a little of the flour. Fold in the remaining flour and the baking powder, then the dried fruit and rosemary. Put the mixture in the prepared tin and smooth the top.

Cook in the centre of a moderate oven (160C, 325 F, gas 3) for about 1½ hours, then reduce the oven temperature to cool (150C, 300 F, gas 2) and continue cooking for a further 1 hour, or until cake is cooked. Test if the cake is cooked by piercing the centre with a skewer; it should come out clean if the cake is done.

Cool the cake in the tin for 30 minutes, then turn it out onto a wire rack and peel off the paper. Leave to cool completely. MAKES 1 (20-CM/8-IN) CAKE.

STRAWBERRY TARTS

Pastry	1 tablespoon plain flour
150 g/5 oz plain flour	150 ml/¼ pint single cream
50 g/2 oz caster sugar	¼ teaspoon vanilla essence
75 g/3 oz butter, cut into small pieces	15 g/½ oz butter
	To finish
1 egg yolk	225 g/8 oz strawberries
Pastry Cream	3 tablespoons redcurrant jelly
1 egg, separated	1 tablespoon water
25 g/1 oz caster sugar	

HEAP the flour on a board and make a well in centre. Add the sugar, butter and egg yolk. Using the fingers of one hand, gradually knead the flour into the butter and egg yolk to form a firm dough. Knead lightly, then chill for 30 minutes.

Roll out the pastry and use it to line 12 deep tartlet tins. Press the pastry well down into tins, prick all over and bake in a moderately hot oven (190 C, 375 F, gas 5) for 10 to 15 minutes, or until golden brown. Turn out and leave to cool on a wire rack.

Meanwhile, make the pastry cream: place the egg yolk and sugar in a basin and whisk until thick and creamy, then add the flour and 1 tablespoon of the cream and mix well. Heat the remaining cream and the vanilla essence until almost boiling, then pour on to the egg yolk mixture. Mix well, then pour back into saucepan, bring to the boil and cook for 1 minute. Whisk in the butter. Remove from the heat and allow to cool, stirring occasionally to prevent a skin forming. Whisk the egg white until stiff but not dry, then fold it into the pastry cream and leave until quite cold.

When the pastry cream is cold, divide it between the six tartlet cases. Arrange the hulled strawberries in each tart. Heat the redcurrant jelly with the water until it has melted. Spoon this glaze over the strawberries in the tarts.

Allow the tarts to cool before serving. MAKES 12.

Variation
Kumquat Tarts: Cook 225 g/8 oz fresh kumquats in 150 ml/
¼ pint water until tender, about 20 minutes. Stir in 50 g/2 oz
caster sugar and set aside.

Make the tartlets as in the main recipe. Lift the
kumquats out of their cooking liquid and arrange them in
the tartlets. Boil the liquid until thick and syrup-like, and
reduced by half. Cool, then spoon over the fruit.

CHIVE AND CHEESE CRISPIES

50 g/2 oz butter
75 g/3 oz Cheddar cheese,
  grated
50 g/2 oz plain potato crisps,
  crushed
50 g/2 oz plain flour

generous pinch of dry
  mustard
1 tablespoon chopped fresh
  chives
salt and pepper

MELT the butter in a small saucepan. Remove from the
heat and add the cheese, crushed crisps, flour, mustard,
chives and seasoning. Roll the mixture into walnut-sized
balls and place the balls on two greased baking trays,
flattening them with a fork.

Bake in a moderate oven (180C, 350F, gas 4) for 12 to 15
minutes, or until crisp. Lift off the crispies and allow to cool
on a wire rack.

Serve these tasty snacks with drinks or as an accompaniment for soup. MAKES ABOUT 20.

PEANUT PICNIC BARS

250 g/9 oz smooth peanut butter	8 tablespoons golden syrup
175 g/6 oz soft light brown sugar	pinch of salt
	1 teaspoon vanilla essence
	65 g/2½ oz Rice Krispies

PUT the peanut butter, sugar, golden syrup, salt and vanilla essence in a large, heatproof bowl over a saucepan of simmering water. Stir the mixture until melted. Remove from the heat and mix in the Rice Krispies.

Spread the mixture in an 18 × 28-cm/7 × 11-in Swiss roll tin and press down firmly. Leave until cold, then cut into 14 bars. MAKES 14.

SEEDLESS RASPBERRY AND REDCURRANT JAM

1.5 kg/3 lb raspberries	2 kg/4½ lb granulated or preserving sugar
450 g/1 lb redcurrants	
300 ml/½ pint water	

PLACE the raspberries, redcurrants and water in a preserving pan, removing any large stalks and leaves. Stir over a low heat until the juices begin to run, then simmer until very soft, about 20 minutes. Remove from the heat and turn the fruit out into a bowl. Rinse out the preserving pan and then press the raspberries and redcurrants through a sieve into the rinsed pan. Add the sugar and stir over a low heat until the sugar has dissolved. Bring to the boil and boil rapidly for 3 to 4 minutes, then test for setting (see page 124). When a soft set has been reached, remove from the heat and allow to cool. Pot the jam, cover with waxed paper and label. Store in a cool place. MAKES ABOUT 2.75 KG/6 LB.

TOMATO AND ONION CHUTNEY

450 g/1 lb ripe, firm
  tomatoes
1 kg/2 lb cooking apples
300 ml/½ pint pickling
  vinegar
1 kg/2 lb granulated sugar
15 g/½ oz ground ginger

15 g/½ oz white mustard
  seeds
2 teaspoons salt
450 g/1 lb onions, finely
  chopped
450 g/1 lb sultanas, chopped

COVER the tomatoes with boiling water, leave them to soak for 30 seconds, then drain and slip off the skins. Roughly chop the tomatoes.

Peel, core and chop the apples and place them in a preserving pan with half the vinegar. Bring to the boil and simmer until the apples are very soft. Add the sugar, remaining vinegar, ginger, mustard seeds, salt and tomatoes. Bring to the boil again and cook rapidly, stirring occasionally, until the mixture has reduced by half. Add the onions and sultanas, bring the mixture back to the boil, stirring constantly. Remove from the heat and allow to cool, then pot and cover.

Label and store in a cool, dark place. MAKES ABOUT 2.75 KG/6 LB.

LEMONADE

2 lemons	450 g/1 lb granulated sugar
15 g/½ oz citric acid	600 ml/1 pint boiling water

SCRUB the lemons and, using a sharp knife or potato peeler, very thinly pare off the peel and place it in a large jug. Squeeze the lemons and add the juice to the jug, with the citric acid and sugar. Pour on the boiling water and stir until the sugar has dissolved. Strain and bottle the lemonade.

Lemonade can be stored in the refrigerator for up to two weeks. MAKES 900 ML/1½ PINTS.

SPARKLING STRAWBERRY PUNCH

450 g/1 lb strawberries	2 tablespoons lemon juice
50 g/2 oz icing sugar	2 bottles sparkling dry white
1 sherry glass of Grand Marnier	wine

HULL the strawberries. Reserve about six for decoration and place the remainder in a liquidiser or food processor. Add the icing sugar, Grand Marnier and lemon juice. Blend until puréed, then pour into a large bowl.

Just before serving, pour on the chilled white wine and add the sliced, reserved strawberries. SERVES 20.

—— AUTUMN ——

As the evenings draw in and the warm days of summer give way to the cool winds of autumn, the fruits of the harvest season are plentiful. By tradition, this is the time of year to enjoy roast pork, shellfish dishes and game; or for preserving fruits and vegetables in jams and chutneys. By necessity, warming soups and casseroles, and satisfying puddings take the place of light summer salads and airy mousses.

Here is a collection of wholesome recipes for everyday meals as well as some which are better suited to dinner parties or a special Sunday lunch. For the Guy Fawkes celebrations you may like to try some of the baked potatoes with Savoury Toad-in-the-hole. A basket of freshly made Drop Scones would bring any bonfire evening to a satisfying end.

SEAFOOD CHOWDER

Fish Stock
225 g/8 oz coley
1 large onion
bay leaf
few sprigs each of parsley,
 thyme, lemon balm and
 oregano
1.75 litres/3 pints water
For the Soup
1 medium onion
2 celery sticks
2 medium carrots
25 g/1 oz butter
4 tablespoons flour

salt and pepper
450 g/1 lb mussels
150 ml/¼ pint dry white wine
450 g/1 lb cod fillet
150 ml/¼ pint milk
225 g/8 oz peeled, cooked
 prawns
50 g/2 oz button mushrooms
4 tablespoons chopped
 parsley
Garnish
Croûtons (page 125)
grated rind of ½ lemon

To make the stock cut the coley into chunks and put these in a saucepan with the onion. Tie the bay leaf with the herbs and add to the pan with the water. Bring to the boil, reduce the heat slightly, cover, and cook for 1 hour. Uncover and boil for a few minutes to reduce the stock to about half its original volume. Strain through a fine sieve and measure the liquid: if there is significantly more than 900 ml/1½ pints, boil the liquid in an open pan to reduce it further.

Chop the onion, thinly slice the celery and dice the carrots. Melt the butter in a large saucepan, add the vegetables and cook for 3 or 4 minutes, or until the onion is soft but not browned. Stir in the flour with a little seasoning and cook for a few minutes, then pour in the stock, stirring all the time. Bring to the boil, reduce the heat, cover and simmer for 30 minutes.

Meanwhile, thoroughly scrub the mussels and remove their beards. Discard any that are open and do not shut when firmly tapped. Put them in a large pan with the wine and bring to the boil. Cover immediately, reduce the heat and simmer for 5 minutes, or until the mussels open. Discard any closed shellfish, then scrape the mussels from their shells into the wine. Discard the shells. (You may like to reserve a few mussels in their shells for garnish.)

Skin the cod and cut it into chunks. Add the milk to the soup with the prawns and mushrooms. Heat through but do not boil, then stir in the cod and poach gently, uncovered, for 15 minutes, or until the fish is cooked.

Finally, stir in the mussels with their cooking liquor, taking care not to break up the fish.

Sprinkle in the parsley and serve hot. Toss the Croûtons with the lemon rind and use to garnish the soup. SERVES 4 TO 6.

CHESHIRE BROCCOLI SOUP

1 large onion	600 ml/1 pint chicken stock
25 g/1 oz butter	300 ml/½ pint milk
1 large potato	salt and pepper
450 g/1 lb broccoli	100 g/4 oz Cheshire cheese

CHOP the onion. Melt the butter in a saucepan, add the onion and cook until soft but not browned, about 3 or 4 minutes. Meanwhile, dice the potato and roughly chop the broccoli. Add these to the onion and cook, stirring, for a few more minutes. Pour in the stock and bring to the boil. Reduce the heat, cover and simmer for 45 minutes.

Blend the soup in a liquidiser. Return it to the rinsed-out pan and add the milk. Heat through without boiling, then taste and season as necessary. Crumble the cheese as finely as possible.

Pour the soup into bowls, then top each portion with a pile of crumbled Cheshire cheese. Serve immediately. SERVES 4.

CREAM OF ARTICHOKE SOUP

450 g/1 lb Jerusalem artichokes	600 ml/1 pint chicken stock
1 large onion	salt and pepper
25 g/1 oz butter	300 ml/½ pint single cream
bay leaf	4 tablespoons chopped parsley
2 tablespoons flour	

PEEL and halve or quarter the artichokes. Put them in a bowl of water as they are peeled, to prevent discoloration. Chop the onion. Melt the butter in a saucepan, add the bay leaf and cook for a minute. Stir in the artichokes and onion and cook until the onion is soft but not brown, about 3 or 4 minutes.

Discard the bay leaf, stir in the flour and gradually pour in the stock, stirring constantly. Bring to the boil, reduce the heat, cover and simmer for 30 minutes, or until the artichokes are broken down slightly.

Blend the soup in a liquidiser, then return it to the rinsed-out saucepan and add seasoning to taste. Re-heat until almost boiling and then remove from the heat to stir in the cream. Heat for a few more minutes but do not boil.

Stir in the parsley and serve hot, with warmed dinner rolls or Melba Toast (see page 125). SERVES 4.

HARVEST SOUP

1 medium onion	bay leaf
1 large leek	2 tablespoons flour
2 large carrots	1.15 litres/2 pints chicken or
1 large potato	bacon stock
1 large parsnip	450 g/1 lb tomatoes
4 celery sticks	4 tablespoons chopped
¼ medium cabbage	parsley
25 g/1 oz butter	salt and pepper

CHOP the onion, trim and slice the leek, dice the carrots, potato, parsnip and celery and shred the cabbage.

Melt the butter in a large saucepan. Add the bay leaf and all the vegetables apart from the cabbage. Cook, stirring frequently, for 3 or 4 minutes until the onion is softened slightly. Stir in the flour, then gradually pour in the stock, still stirring. Bring to the boil, then reduce the heat and cover the pan. Simmer the soup for 25 minutes.

While the soup is simmering, put the tomatoes in a large bowl and pour on boiling water to cover. Leave for 30 to 60 seconds, then drain and peel. Cut the tomatoes into quarters, discard the seeds, then roughly chop them up.

Add the cabbage, tomatoes and parsley to the soup and simmer for a further 10 minutes, or until all the vegetables are tender.

Serve some warmed, crusty bread with the soup. SERVES 6.

Variation
Minestrone Soup: Add 2 crushed cloves of garlic to the soup with the bay leaf. Continue as above, then add 50 g/ 2 oz short-cut macaroni after the soup has simmered for 15 to 20 minutes. Double the quantity of tomatoes.

Serve some freshly grated Parmesan cheese with the minestrone.

CELERY AND BACON SOUP

225 g/8 oz rindless lean (streaky) bacon	900 ml/1½ pints chicken or ham stock
1 large onion	150 ml/¼ pint single cream
1 medium potato	salt and pepper
1 head of celery	3 tablespoons chopped parsley
1 tablespoon flour	

CHOP the bacon and onion. Roughly chop the potato. Trim and slice the celery. Dry fry the bacon in a heavy-based saucepan until the fat runs, then continue to cook until the bacon is crisp and browned. Use a slotted spoon to remove the bacon from the pan. Drain it thoroughly on absorbent kitchen paper and set aside. Reserve the fat.

Add the vegetables to the bacon fat and cook gently until the onion is soft but not browned, about 3 or 4 minutes. Stir in the flour and cook for 1 minute, then gradually pour in the stock and bring to the boil. Reduce the heat, cover and simmer for 45 minutes.

Blend the soup in a liquidiser, then return it to the rinsed-out pan and re-heat. Before the soup reaches boiling point, stir in the cream and heat for a minute or so without boiling. Taste and add seasoning if necessary.

Stir the crisp bacon and parsley into the soup just before it is served. Warmed granary or wholemeal bread goes well with this soup. SERVES 4 TO 6.

GARLIC LENTIL PÂTÉ

1 medium onion	50 g/2 oz cream cheese
25 g/1 oz butter	50 g/2 oz black olives,
2 large cloves garlic,	stoned
crushed	*Garnish*
100 g/4 oz red lentils	lemon wedges
300 ml/½ pint water	black olives
salt and pepper	
2 tablespoons chopped	
parsley	

FINELY chop the onion. Melt the butter in a small sauce-pan, add the onion and garlic and cook until the onion is soft but not browned, about 3 or 4 minutes. Stir in the lentils and water. Add a little seasoning, bring to the boil and reduce the heat. Cover and simmer for 20 to 30 minutes, or until the lentils are tender. Check during cooking to make sure that they are not drying out too much and that they do not stick to the bottom of the pan. At the end of the cooking time, the lentils should have absorbed all the water.

Allow the lentils to cool until they are just warm before beating in the parsley and cream cheese. Roughly chop the olives, stir them into the pâté and taste for seasoning. Put in a small basin and chill thoroughly.

Serve scoops of the pâté on individual plates, garnished with lemon wedges and a few whole olives. Warmed pitta bread or French bread go well with this pâté. SERVES 4.

AUBERGINE FRITTERS
WITH ROQUEFORT CREAM

2 small aubergines	2 eggs, separated
salt and pepper	150 ml/¼ pint water
Batter	oil for deep frying
100 g/4 oz plain flour, plus	*Roquefort Cream*
extra for coating	175 g/6 oz Roquefort cheese
1 teaspoon dried mixed	150 ml/¼ pint soured cream
herbs	1 tablespoon chopped chives

TRIM the ends off the aubergines, then slice them. Lay the slices in a colander or sieve, sprinkling them generously with salt. Set aside over a bowl for 30 to 40 minutes. Wash and thoroughly drain the aubergine slices, then plunge them into a saucepan of boiling, salted water. Bring quickly back to the boil, remove from the heat and drain again. Set aside.

Make the Roquefort cream, allowing time to chill it before serving the fritters. Mash the cheese, gradually adding the soured cream. Stir in the chives and a little pepper, then spoon into a small dish. Cover and chill.

To make the batter: sift the flour into a bowl, adding a generous pinch of salt and the herbs. Make a well in the middle and drop in the egg yolks. Gradually pour in the water, beating constantly, and incorporate the flour a little at a time.

Dust the aubergine slices with flour. Heat the oil to 190C/ 375F. Just before you are ready to cook the fritters, whisk the egg whites until they stand in stiff peaks, stir a spoonful into the batter, then carefully fold in the rest.

Dip the floured aubergine slices into the batter, then lower them into the hot oil and cook until crisp and golden. Drain on absorbent kitchen paper and serve hot with the Roquefort cream. SERVES 4.

STILTON AND APPLE STUFFED ONIONS

4 large onions (about 225 g/
  8 oz each)
225 g/8 oz cooking apples
100 g/4 oz fresh
  breadcrumbs

100 g/4 oz blue Stilton
  cheese
1 bunch watercress
salt and pepper
50 g/2 oz butter

PEEL the onions, then cook them in a large pan of boiling water for 15 minutes, until they are just tender. Drain and allow to cool until they can be handled.

Peel, core and chop the apples. Mix with the breadcrumbs. Finely crumble the cheese and add to the mixture. Reserve four sprigs of the watercress for garnish, then trim and chop the rest and add it to the cheese mixture.

Remove the middle of each onion – this is easiest if you gradually scoop out the layers of onion with a teaspoon. Leave an unbroken shell about two layers thick. Chop the scooped-out onion and add the cheese mixture. Mix well and add seasoning to taste, then press the mixture into the onion shells.

Stand the onions in an ovenproof dish and dot the top of each with a little butter. Bake in a moderate oven (180 C, 350 F, gas 4) for 35 to 40 minutes, or until the stuffing is cooked through.

Serve on individual plates, garnished with the reserved watercress. SERVES 4.

HOT TOMATO STARTER

8 medium tomatoes	salt and pepper
1 medium onion	2 tablespoons grated
75 g/3 oz butter	Parmesan cheese
1 large clove garlic, crushed	2 tablespoons finely
100 g/4 oz fresh	chopped, blanched
breadcrumbs	almonds (optional)
4 tablespoons chopped	parsley sprigs to garnish
parsley	

PUT the tomatoes in a large bowl and pour on boiling water to cover. Leave for 30 to 60 seconds, then drain and peel. Cut the tomatoes in half, scoop out the seeds and set aside. Finely chop the onion.

Melt two-thirds of the butter in a saucepan. Add the onion and cook until soft but not brown, about 3 or 4 minutes. Stir in the garlic, breadcrumbs and parsley. Add seasoning to taste and continue to cook over a low heat until hot, then remove from the heat.

Beat the Parmesan cheese and almonds (if used) into the remaining butter. Divide the breadcrumb mixture between the tomatoes. Turn the tomatoes cut side downwards on to four individual, ovenproof dishes. Top each with a little of the Parmesan mixture and put under a hot grill until lightly browned on top. Serve immediately, garnished with parsley. SERVES 4.

NOTE: Allowing 2 tomatoes per person this will make a substantial starter. If you are serving a filling main course, then halve the quantities. The hot tomatoes are delicious for lunch and make an excellent accompaniment to creamy scrambled eggs.

COD AND LEEK COBBLER

1 large red pepper
3 large leeks
25 g/1 oz butter
2 tablespoons flour
salt and pepper
1 quantity fish stock (page 62)
100 g/4 oz mushrooms, sliced
1 kg/2 lb cod or haddock
　fillet
50 g/2 oz fresh breadcrumbs
50 g/2 oz matured Cheddar
　cheese, grated

Scone Topping
100 g/4 oz self-raising flour
1 teaspoon baking powder
4 tablespoons chopped
　parsley
1 teaspoon dried mixed
　herbs
25 g/1 oz butter
4 or 5 tablespoons milk, plus
　extra for glazing

CUT the top off the pepper, remove the seeds and pith from inside and chop the shell. Trim and slice the leeks. Melt the butter in a saucepan, add the pepper and leeks and cook for 3 or 4 minutes to soften the pepper. Stir in the flour, with a little seasoning. Gradually pour in the stock, stirring constantly, and bring to the boil. Remove from the heat and stir in the mushrooms.

Skin the fish and cut it into chunks. Add these to the leek mixture, stirring lightly. Turn the mixture into an ovenproof dish. Mix the breadcrumbs and cheese and sprinkle over the centre of the dish.

To make the scones: sift the flour into a bowl and stir in the baking powder, parsley and herbs. Rub in the butter, then stir in the milk to make a soft dough. Turn out on to a floured surface, knead together very lightly and roll out to 1 cm/½ in thick. Cut out eight 3.5–5-cm/1½–2-in rounds.

Lay the scones on top of the fish mixture, overlapping them round the edge of the dish. Brush with a little milk to glaze and bake in a moderately hot oven (190 C, 375 F, gas 5) for 30 minutes, or until the fish is cooked and the scones are risen and browned. Serve piping hot. SERVES 4.

CELERIAC-STUFFED COD STEAKS

1 small celeriac
50 g/2 oz butter
50 g/2 oz fresh breadcrumbs
50 g/2 oz Lancashire,
   Cheshire or Caerphilly
   cheese, grated or finely
   crumbled
2 tablespoons chopped
   parsley

2 tablespoons chopped fresh
   chives
2 tablespoons chopped fresh
   dill
salt and pepper
4 cod steaks
Garnish
parsley sprigs
lemon slices

PEEL the celeriac and cut it into chunks. Cook it in boiling, salted water for 15 to 20 minutes, or until tender. Drain and mash, beat in half the butter, then add the breadcrumbs, cheese, herbs and seasoning.

Carefully remove the bones from the middle of the cod steaks and place the fish in a greased, ovenproof dish. Spoon the celeriac mixture into the cavities left by the bones and on top of the fish steaks. Dot with the remaining butter. Bake in a moderately hot oven (200 C, 400 F, gas 6) for 40 minutes, or until the fish is cooked and the celeriac mixture is browned.

Serve immediately, garnished with parsley sprigs and lemon slices. SERVES 4.

SMOKED HADDOCK AND SPINACH GRATIN

1 kg/2 lb fresh spinach	2 tablespoons chopped
salt and pepper	parsley
50 g/2 oz butter	100 g/4 oz Emmental or
a little grated nutmeg	Gruyère cheese, finely
675 g/1½ lb smoked haddock	grated
fillet	50 g/2 oz fresh breadcrumbs
2 quantities Basic White	
Sauce (page 126)	

TRIM the stalks from the spinach, wash thoroughly and shake off the excess water. Put the damp spinach in a large saucepan, cover and heat gently at first, then more quickly as the vegetable begins to cook. Shake the pan and stir occasionally until the spinach is cooked, about 3 minutes. Drain thoroughly and chop. Beat in a little salt and pepper with the butter, and nutmeg to taste.

Spread the spinach in a greased, ovenproof dish. Skin the haddock and cut it into pieces. Place the pieces on top of the spinach. Make the Basic White Sauce, then beat in the parsley and two-thirds of the cheese. Pour the sauce over the fish. Mix the breadcrumbs with the reserved cheese and sprinkle over the top.

Bake the gratin in a moderately hot oven (200 C, 400 F, gas 6) for 30 to 40 minutes, or until the fish is cooked and the topping is crisp and golden. Serve freshly cooked, with rice or pasta. SERVES 4.

MUSSELS WITH LEEKS AND TOMATOES

1 kg/2 lb mussels	grated rind of ½ lemon
450 g/1 lb leeks	bay leaf
450 g/1 lb tomatoes	300 ml/½ pint dry white wine
75 g/3 oz butter	2 tablespoons flour
salt and pepper	2 tablespoons chopped
1 large clove garlic, crushed	parsley

THOROUGHLY scrub the mussels, scraping off the beards. Discard any that are open and do not shut when firmly tapped.

Trim and thinly slice the leeks. Put the tomatoes in a large bowl and pour on boiling water to cover. Leave for 30 to 60 seconds, then drain, peel and chop.

Melt two-thirds of the butter in a large saucepan. Add the leeks, a little seasoning and the garlic and cook, stirring occasionally, for 2 or 3 minutes. Stir in the lemon rind, bay leaf and wine. Add the mussels and bring to the boil. Cover the pan immediately and simmer for about 5 minutes, or until the mussels have all opened. Discard any that have not opened.

Beat the remaining butter with the flour until smooth. Scoop the mussels out of the pan using a slotted spoon, and transfer them to warmed serving bowls. Discard the bay leaf. Add knobs of the butter and flour mixture to the cooking liquor and stir over a high heat until the liquor boils. Reduce the heat, stir in the tomatoes and the parsley and cook for 1 minute.

Pour this sauce over the mussels and serve immediately. Serve some warmed French bread with the mussels. SERVES 4.

SCALLOPS WITH ALMOND SAUCE

12 scallops, cleaned
1 small onion
25 g/1 oz butter
50 g/2 oz blanched almonds
300 ml/½ pint dry white wine

100 g/4 oz button
  mushrooms
2 tablespoons chopped
  parsley
4 tablespoons single cream

HALVE the scallops and set aside. Finely chop the onion. Melt the butter in a saucepan, add the onion and almonds and cook until the onion is soft, about 3 or 4 minutes. Pour in the white wine and bring to the boil. Reduce the heat, cover and simmer for 20 minutes. Thinly slice the mushrooms.

Blend the sauce in a liquidiser until smooth, then press through a sieve to remove any grainy bits of almond. Pour the sauce back into the rinsed-out saucepan. Heat slowly to boiling point, reduce the heat and add the scallops. Poach gently for 3 to 5 minutes, or until cooked. Stir in the parsley and mushrooms. Heat for 1 minute, then add the cream.

Serve with tiny pasta shells or creamy mashed potatoes. SERVES 4.

ROAST CHICKEN
WITH APPLE AND APRICOT STUFFING

1 (1.5-kg/3½-lb) oven-ready chicken	1 medium onion
Stuffing	1 teaspoon dried thyme
1 large cooking apple	1 teaspoon dried sage
100 g/4 oz dried apricots	salt and pepper
100 g/4 oz fresh breadcrumbs	4 tablespoons brandy or dry sherry
	2 tablespoons orange juice

TRIM any excess fat from the chicken and scald the inside.

To make the stuffing: peel, core and finely chop the apple, chop the apricots and mix both with the breadcrumbs. Finely chop the onion and add to the fruit mixture with the herbs, seasoning, brandy or sherry and orange juice. Mix well to make a moist stuffing.

Spoon the stuffing into the chicken, pressing it in well. Tie the legs and wings securely in place, to give a good shape, then roast the bird in a moderate oven (180 C, 350 F, gas 4) for 1½ hours, or until cooked through. If the top of the chicken looks slightly dry during the first part of the cooking time, dot it with a little butter or brush with a little oil. Later, as the chicken makes its own juices, baste the bird once or twice. When cooked, the juices will run clear if the bird is pricked; test the meat on the thick part of the thigh to make sure.

Serve with roast potatoes and a selection of simply cooked vegetables. SERVES 4.

CHICKEN IN THE POT

1 large onion	bay leaf
2 leeks	2 or 3 sprigs thyme
4 celery sticks	2 sprigs rosemary
4 large carrots	2 or 3 parsley sprigs
4 large potatoes	1.15 litres/2 pints dry cider
4 rashers rindless streaky	salt and pepper
bacon	25 g/1 oz butter
1 (1.5-kg/3½-lb) oven-ready	3 tablespoons flour
chicken	

THICKLY slice the onion, leeks, celery and carrots. Cut the potatoes into chunks. Roughly chop the bacon and put it in a very large saucepan or flameproof dish. Heat gently until the fat runs, then increase the heat and add the onion. Cook until soft, about 3 or 4 minutes.

Remove the onion and bacon from the pan, using a slotted spoon, then brown the chicken all over in the remaining fat. Replace the onion and bacon, add the herbs and pour in the cider. Sprinkle in seasoning, to taste.

Bring to the boil, reduce the heat so that the liquid is simmering steadily and cover the pan. Cook for 1 hour. Add the leeks, celery, carrots and potatoes and simmer for a further 20 minutes, or until the chicken is cooked and the vegetables are tender.

Remove the chicken and vegetables, transferring them to a large, heated serving platter. Discard the bay leaf and herb sprigs. Beat the butter and flour together until smooth, then add knobs of this mixture to the liquid in the pan. Heat, stirring constantly, until the liquid boils. Cook for 1 or 2 minutes, or until thickened.

Serve the chicken with the gravy and vegetables. SERVES 4 TO 6.

CHICKEN AND GAMMON GOUGÈRE

2 boneless chicken breasts	300 ml/½ pint milk
1 (350-g/12-oz) gammon joint	salt and pepper
	Choux Pastry
1 large onion	300 ml/½ pint water
2 tablespoons oil	100 g/4 oz butter
100 g/4 oz button mushrooms	175 g/6 oz plain flour
	4 eggs
2 tablespoons flour	2 tablespoons chopped parsley
1 chicken stock cube	
300 ml/½ pint water	1 tablespoon dried tarragon

CUT the chicken breasts into bite-sized chunks. Trim the gammon and cut it into similar-sized pieces. Slice the onion. Heat the oil in a large frying pan or heavy-based saucepan. Quickly fry the onion with the chicken and gammon, until the meats are lightly browned. Add the mushrooms and flour, stir well and add the stock cube. Pour in the water and milk, stirring constantly. Bring to the boil, season lightly and set aside.

To make the choux pastry: put the water and butter into a saucepan. Heat gently until the butter melts, then bring quickly to the boil and tip in all the flour. Remove the pan from the heat. Beat well, so that the ingredients form a thick paste which comes away from the sides of the pan in a smooth ball. Leave to cool slightly before beating in the eggs and herbs. Continue beating until the paste is very smooth and glossy.

Pipe or spoon the choux pastry round the edge of a greased, ovenproof dish, then ladle the chicken and gammon mixture into the centre. Bake in a hot oven (220 C, 425 F, gas 7) for 20 minutes, then reduce the temperature to moderately hot (190 C, 375 F, gas 5) and cook for a further 40 to 45 minutes, or until the choux pastry is well puffed, golden and crisp. Serve immediately. SERVES 4 TO 6.

DUCK WITH PLUMS

1 (1.75-kg/4-lb) oven-ready duck	salt and pepper
1 large onion, quartered	450 g/1 lb plums
bay leaf	3 tablespoons flour
cinnamon stick	300 ml/½ pint duck or chicken stock
4 cloves	150 ml/¼ pint port

CUT away any lumps of fat from inside the duck. Put the onion, bay leaf and spices in the body cavity. Rub the outside of the duck all over with salt and thoroughly prick the skin.

Put the duck in a roasting tin and cook in a moderately hot oven (200 C, 400 F, gas 6) for 1½ hours, or until well browned and crisp. Test to make sure that the bird is cooked through, by piercing the flesh at the thickest part of the thigh: the juice should run clear.

Meanwhile, halve the plums and remove their stones. Lift the duck out of the tin and drain it of all fat. Transfer it to a serving platter and keep hot. Drain off the fat from the tin, then stir the flour into the cooking juices. Cook over a low heat for a few minutes, then pour in the stock, stirring constantly, and bring to the boil. Cook gently for a few minutes, stirring all the roasted sediment off the pan. Add the port and plums, then cook for a few more minutes. Add a little pepper if necessary.

The duck can be served whole, to be carved at the table, or it can be cut into joints and served on individual plates, with some of the sauce poured over the top. SERVES 4.

ROAST PHEASANT
WITH ORANGE AND RAISIN SAUCE

2 medium pheasants (preferably hen birds, as these are more tender than cocks)	300 ml/½ pint red wine
	25 g/1 oz raisins
	1 tablespoon flour
	25 g/1 oz butter
6 rashers fatty streaky bacon	150 ml/¼ pint chicken or
pared rind and juice of 1 large orange	game stock
	salt and pepper

PLACE the pheasants in a roasting tin. Lay three rashers of bacon over each bird, to prevent them from drying out during cooking. Roast the pheasants in a moderately hot oven (200 C, 400 F, gas 6) for 1–1¼ hours, or until tender.

Cut the orange rind into very fine strips. Put this, with the orange juice and a little of the red wine, into the roasting tin about 20 minutes before the end of the cooking time. Soak the raisins in the rest of the red wine until the birds are cooked. Beat the flour into the butter to make a smooth paste.

When the pheasants are cooked, transfer them to a warmed serving dish and keep hot. Pour the wine and raisins, and the stock into the roasting tin. Heat gently, stirring all the time to incorporate the cooking sediment from the roasting tin. When the sauce reaches boiling point, reduce the heat so that it simmers very gently for 2 to 3 minutes, or until the raisins are quite plump.

Stirring all the time, add knobs of the butter and flour mixture. When the butter has all melted, bring the sauce to the boil and cook for a few minutes. Season before serving.

Remove the bacon from the pheasants before they are served. Pour the sauce over the birds and serve at once. SERVES 4.

CASSEROLE OF PHEASANT
WITH JUNIPER AND APPLE

225 g/8 oz rindless streaky
   bacon, chopped
2 tablespoons juniper
   berries, crushed
2 medium pheasants (the
   less tender cocks are
   suitable for this recipe)
4 tablespoons brandy or
   Calvados (French apple
   brandy)

225 g/8 oz pickling onions
2 celery sticks, sliced
bay leaf
salt and pepper
4 tablespoons flour
1 bottle red wine
4 Cox's Orange Pippin
   apples
25 g/1 oz butter

HEAT the bacon in a large, heavy-based frying pan until
the fat runs and the bacon is crisp. Use a slotted spoon to
remove the bacon from the pan, set aside. Reserve the fat.

Add the juniper berries to the fat in the pan, cook for 1
minute, then add the pheasants and cook until brown all
over. Lift the birds into a large, ovenproof casserole dish,
then sprinkle over the bacon and the juniper berries. In a
separate pan, warm the brandy or Calvados, pour it over
the birds and ignite immediately.

Add the onions, celery and bay leaf to the fat remaining
in the frying pan and cook for 3 or 4 minutes, until slightly
softened. Stir in seasoning and the flour, then gradually
pour in the wine, stirring all the time to prevent lumps
forming. Bring to the boil, then pour into the pheasant
casserole and cover tightly. Cook in a moderate oven
(180 C, 350 F, gas 4) for $1\frac{1}{4}$ to $1\frac{1}{2}$ hours, or until the birds are
cooked and tender.

Meanwhile, core and slice the apples into rings. Melt the
butter in a frying pan, and brown the apples over a fairly
high heat. Drain the apple slices on absorbent kitchen
paper and add them to the casserole just before it is served.
SERVES 4.

CORIANDER PORK AND PARSNIPS

675 g/1½ lb lean, boneless
    pork (cut from the leg,
    hand or knuckle)
1 tablespoon coriander
    seeds, coarsely crushed
2 tablespoons oil
1 large onion, chopped
salt and pepper

bay leaf
4 tablespoons flour
2 tablespoons Dijon mustard
450 ml/¾ pint chicken stock
450 g/1 lb parsnips
3 or 4 tablespoons chopped
    parsley

CUT the pork into bite-sized cubes. Heat the oil in a heavy-based saucepan, add the pork and coriander seeds, and cook until all the pieces are evenly browned. Stir in the onion, reduce the heat slightly and cook for 3 or 4 minutes. Sprinkle in salt and pepper and add the bay leaf, then stir in the flour, mustard and stock, stirring all the time to prevent lumps forming. Bring to the boil, reduce the heat, cover and simmer very gently for 15 minutes.

Meanwhile, peel and trim the parsnips, then cut them into chunks. Add the pieces to the pork casserole and simmer gently for about 30 minutes, or until the meat and vegetables are cooked. Stir in the parsley just before serving.

Baked potatoes, plain cooked rice or pasta will go well with this casserole. SERVES 4.

SAVOURY TOAD-IN-THE-HOLE

1 large onion	2 large eggs
2 tablespoons oil	300 ml/½ pint milk
100 g/4 oz plain flour	2 tablespoons water
salt and pepper	450 g/1 lb good quality pork
1 tablespoon dried mixed	sausages
herbs	

IT is worth using good quality sausages for this recipe – the better the sausages, the better the toad.

Finely chop the onion, then cook it in 1 tablespoon oil until soft but not browned, about 3 or 4 minutes. Set aside to cool.

Sift the flour and plenty of salt and pepper into a bowl. Stir in the herbs, then make a well in the middle and add the eggs. Gradually beat in the milk, working in the flour to make a smooth batter. Lastly, beat in the water and the cooked onion.

Use the remaining oil to grease a roasting tin or oven-proof dish. Prick the sausages and place them in the tin or dish. Pour in the batter and bake in a moderately hot oven (200 C, 400 F, gas 6) for about 45 minutes, or until the batter is well risen and crisp and the sausages are cooked through. Serve immediately. SERVES 4 TO 6.

BAKED POTATOES

4 large potatoes   butter to serve
salt

THOROUGHLY scrub the potatoes, then prick them all over and rub the skin with salt. Put them in a roasting tin and bake in a moderately hot oven (200 C, 400 F, gas 6) for about 1¼ to 1½ hours, or until the potatoes are tender all the way through.

Serve freshly cooked, with a large cross cut in the top of each, with a knob of butter inserted in the opening. Alternatively, the potatoes can be split open or cut in half and served with any of the following fillings or toppings. All the quantities given are for four potatoes. SERVES 4.

Fillings
Smoked Mackerel and Horseradish Cream: Flake the fish from 2 large smoked mackerel fillets. Very finely slice 1 small onion and mix it with the fish. Grate the rind from ½ lemon, mix with 2 to 4 tablespoons chopped parsley and stir both into the fish mixture. Season with freshly ground black pepper. Divide the fish mixture between the potatoes, then top each with a spoonful of creamed horseradish.

Creamed Chicken and Mushroom: Make 300 ml/½ pint Basic White Sauce (see page 126). Stir in 50 g/2 oz sliced button mushrooms, 225–350 g/8–12 oz chopped cooked chicken and 4 chopped spring onions or fresh parsley. Heat for a few minutes, then divide the mixture between the halved baked potatoes.

Special Sausage and Beans: Finely chop 1 large onion, then cook in 1 tablespoon oil until soft but not brown, about 3 or 4 minutes. Add 1 (425-g/15-oz) can baked beans and heat through. Serve the split potatoes topped with beans and cooked chipolata sausages.

Ratatouille and Mozzarella: Make some ratatouille (over-leaf). Top the split potatoes with a generous portion of ratatouille, then add 3 or 4 slices Mozzarella cheese to each and brown the top under the grill.

Simple Toppings
Cream Cheese with Herbs: Beat chopped parsley, thyme, oregano, sage, rosemary and lemon balm into 175–225 g/6–8 oz cream cheese. Use as many fresh herbs as you can find and add small quantities of dried herbs for additional flavour Shape the herb cheese into a roll and chill until firm. Cut into thick slices, then top each potato with a couple of slices.

Soured Cream with Chives: Probably the easiest topping for potatoes. Stir 4 tablespoons chopped fresh chives into 150 ml/¼ pint soured cream, then spoon the mixture over the freshly cooked potatoes.

Cooked Ham and Tomato: Cut each potato in half, cutting almost all the way through. Roll 4 slices cooked ham and put one on each potato. Cut 4 tomatoes into quarters and arrange the pieces on the potatoes. Sprinkle with chopped parsley and serve with mustard.

Bacon Rolls: Roll 8 rashers rindless lean bacon and thread them on to skewers. Grill until crisp and golden, then top each potato with a couple of bacon rolls. Add watercress to garnish and serve with cream cheese or soured cream.

Cheese and Onion: Coarsely grate 175 g/6 oz matured Cheddar cheese and mix with 1 large chopped onion. Split the potatoes, then divide the cheese mixture between them.

Stilton and Walnut: Crumble 175 g/6 oz blue Stilton cheese. Mix in 100 g/4 oz roughly chopped walnuts and 2 tablespoons chopped fresh chives or parsley. Split the potatoes and divide the Stilton mixture between them.

RATATOUILLE

1 large aubergine	450 g/1 lb tomatoes
salt and pepper	about 150 ml/¼ pint olive oil
1 large onion	2 to 4 large cloves garlic,
1 large green pepper	crushed
1 large red pepper	4 tablespoons chopped
225 g/8 oz courgettes	parsley

TRIM the ends off the aubergine, then slice it. Place the slices in a colander, sprinkling each layer generously with salt. Place over a basin and leave for at least 30 minutes.

Meanwhile, slice the onion. Cut the stalk ends off the peppers, remove the seeds and pith, then slice the shells. Trim and slice the courgettes. Place the tomatoes in a bowl, cover with freshly boiling water and leave for 30 to 60 seconds. Drain and peel the tomatoes, then cut them into quarters.

Rinse and dry the aubergines. Pour a layer of olive oil into a large, flameproof dish. Add the garlic and heat gently. When hot, add the aubergine slices and fry until lightly browned, turn and cook the second side. (You may have to cook the aubergine in two batches.) Remove the aubergine slices from the pan, using a slotted spoon, and set aside. Top up with more oil, as necessary, during cooking.

Add the onion and peppers and cook over a fairly high heat until slightly softened. Stir in the courgettes and tomatoes, then put the aubergine slices back in. Stir very gently to combine the ingredients. Add a little seasoning, cover and simmer for 20 to 30 minutes, depending on how you like vegetables cooked.

Add the parsley just before serving the ratatouille. SERVES 4.

CURRIED CAULIFLOWER AND CARROTS

1 large onion	1 tablespoon concentrated
2 tablespoons oil	tomato purée
2 cloves garlic	salt and pepper
2 tablespoons grated fresh	1 medium cauliflower
root ginger	225 g/8 oz carrots
2 teaspoons curry powder	2 tablespoons chopped fresh
bay leaf	coriander leaves
300 ml/½ pint water or	
chicken stock	

FINELY chop the onion. Heat the oil in a heavy-based saucepan, then add the garlic, ginger and onion. Cook gently, stirring frequently, until the onion is soft but not browned, about 3 or 4 minutes. Stir in the curry powder and bay leaf, then add the water or stock. Stir in the tomato purée and seasoning to taste, and bring to the boil. Reduce the heat, cover and simmer for 3 to 5 minutes.

Meanwhile, separate the cauliflower into florets and trim and slice the carrots. Add both to the pan, making sure they are well coated in sauce. Re-cover the pan and cook the vegetables gently for about 20 to 30 minutes, or until they are just tender. Stir carefully once or twice during cooking.

At the end of the cooking time, uncover the pan and boil for a few minutes to evaporate any excess liquid. The curry should have plenty of sauce but it should not be runny. Sprinkle with coriander just before serving.

This curry can be served to accompany a main dish, or it can be served with plain cooked rice and crisp poppadums to make a light lunch or vegetarian main dish. SERVES 4.

AUTUMN FRUIT DUMPLINGS

1½ quantities Shortcrust
   Pastry (page 126)
4 large cooking apples
225 g/8 oz blackberries
grated rind of 1 orange
4 tablespoons soft light
   brown sugar

½ teaspoon ground cinnamon
milk to glaze
2–4 tablespoons chopped
   hazelnuts

CUT the Shortcrust Pastry into quarters.

Peel and core the apples. Make sure that the blackberries
are free of stalks and perfectly clean. Mix the orange rind
with the sugar and cinnamon, then sprinkle this mixture
over the blackberries and stir lightly.

Roll out the pastry into four large circles. Place an apple
on each and fill the middles with the blackberry mixture.
Use a teaspoon to press the fruit down lightly. Pile any
remaining blackberry mixture on top of the apples.
Dampen the edges of the pastry with water or milk, then
fold it up around the fruit to enclose the apples completely.
Pinch the pastry together firmly to seal in the fruit, then
place the dumplings on a greased baking tray.

Brush the dumplings with a little milk, then press on the
chopped hazelnuts. Bake in a moderately hot oven (200 C,
400 F, gas 6) for about 30 minutes, or until golden. Serve
hot with a custard sauce or cream. SERVES 4.

PEAR AND ALMOND PIE

1½ quantities Sweet Shortcrust Pastry (page 126)
225 g/8 oz ground almonds
50 g/2 oz caster sugar
4 tablespoons rum or sweet
   sherry

4 firm pears
juice of ½ lemon
Glaze
milk
caster sugar

ROLL out two-thirds of the Sweet Shortcrust Pastry and
use it to line an ovenproof tart-plate or flan dish.

Stir the almonds with the sugar and rum or sherry to
make a crumbly mixture. Spoon this mixture over the
pastry base but do not press it down. Peel, core and halve
the pears, then toss them quickly in lemon juice and drain
off all the excess. Arrange the pears on top of the almond
mixture without pressing them down.

Roll out the remaining pastry to make a lid. Dampen the
edges of the pastry base with milk or water, cover with the
freshly rolled pastry and press the edges together well to
seal in the filling. Trim the edges (use the trimmings to
make leaves to decorate the top, if you like). Make a small
hole in the centre to allow steam to escape during cooking.
Brush with milk and sprinkle with a little caster sugar.

Bake the pie in a moderately hot oven (200 C, 400 F, gas
6) for 15 minutes, then reduce the oven temperature to
moderate (180 C, 350 F, gas 4) and cook for a further 25 to 30
minutes. Serve hot with cream. SERVES 6.

BLACKCURRANT FLAN

1 quantity Sweet Shortcrust Pastry (page 126)	2 tablespoons Cassis
	Topping
450 g/1 lb blackcurrants	2 large egg whites
50 g/2 oz sugar	75 g/3 oz caster sugar
2 teaspoons cornflour	100 g/4 oz ground almonds
2 tablespoons water	25 g/1 oz nibbed almonds

ROLL out the Sweet Shortcrust Pastry and use to line a 20–23-cm/8–9-in flan dish. Prick the base all over, then line with a large piece of greaseproof paper. Sprinkle baking beans over the base of the flan and bake in a moderately hot oven (200 C, 400 F, gas 6) for 15 minutes. Carefully remove the peas or beans and the paper, then cook for a further 10 to 15 minutes, or until the centre is cooked.

Meanwhile, string the currants and put them in a saucepan with the sugar. Heat gently until the juice runs, then continue to poach the fruit for about 5 minutes or until it is just soft. Blend the cornflour with the water and add to the blackcurrants, stirring all the time. Bring to the boil, add the Cassis, then remove the pan from the heat.

Pour the fruit into the flan case. For the topping, whisk the egg whites until they stand in stiff peaks. Whisking all the time, gradually add the sugar and continue whisking hard until the mixture is smooth and very glossy. Fold in the ground almonds.

Swirl this macaroon topping over the fruit to cover it completely. Sprinkle with the nibbed almonds and put in a moderate oven (180 C, 350 F, gas 4) and cook for about 25 to 30 minutes or until browned.

Serve at once, with some whipped cream if you like. SERVES 6 TO 8.

SIMPLE SESAME PLAIT

450 g/1 lb strong white flour,
   wholewheat flour or
   granary flour
1 teaspoon salt
50 g/2 oz butter or
   margarine
1 sachet easy-blend yeast

300 ml/½ pint lukewarm
   water
Glaze
1 egg, beaten
2 tablespoons unroasted
   sesame seeds

SIFT the flour into a bowl with the salt. Rub in the butter or margarine, then stir in the yeast. Make a well in the centre and pour in the water. Gradually mix the water into the flour, to make an elastic dough. Turn the dough out on to a floured surface and knead thoroughly for about 10 minutes, or until it is very smooth and elastic.

Place the dough in a floured bowl, cover with cling film and leave in a warm place until doubled in size, about 45 to 60 minutes. Turn the risen dough out on to a floured surface, knead lightly and divide into three equal pieces.

Roll the pieces of dough into long strips (about 38 cm/ 15 in. in length), then plait these together on a greased baking tray. Cover with a piece of lightly oiled cling film and leave in a warm place until doubled in size, this time about 30 minutes.

Brush the risen loaf with a little beaten egg and sprinkle generously with sesame seeds, then bake in a hot oven (220 C, 425 F, gas 7) for 35 to 40 minutes, or until golden brown. To test if the bread is cooked, protect your hand with a clean tea-towel and turn the loaf upside down. When tapped on the bottom, the bread should sound hollow. Leave to cool on a wire rack. MAKES 1 LARGE LOAF.

DROP SCONES

100 g/4 oz plain flour	1 egg, beaten
pinch of salt	150 ml/¼ pint milk
25 g/1 oz butter	butter or oil for cooking
1 teaspoon cream of tartar	*To serve*
½ teaspoon bicarbonate of	melted butter
soda	caster sugar

SIFT the flour into a bowl with the salt, then rub in the butter. Stir in the cream of tartar and the bicarbonate of soda, then make a well in the centre. Add the egg and gradually beat in the milk to make a very smooth, thick batter.

Heat a griddle and grease it with a little butter or oil. Have ready a warmed tea-towel on a large plate. Drop spoonfuls of the batter in small circles on to the hot griddle. Cook until the underside is set and the top of the drop scones are bubbling. Use a palette knife to turn the scones and cook until golden on the second side.

Transfer the scones to the hot tea-towel and serve brushed generously with melted butter and sprinkled with a little caster sugar. MAKES ABOUT 12.

PEAR AND GINGER CHUTNEY

1 kg/2 lb firm pears	175 g/6 oz soft dark brown
3 large onions	sugar
75 g/3 oz raisins	300 ml/½ pint vinegar
2 tablespoons fresh root	½ teaspoon salt
ginger, finely chopped	cinnamon stick

PEEL, core and roughly chop the pears. Chop the onions. Put both in a large saucepan with the raisins. Add all the remaining ingredients and bring slowly to the boil, stirring occasionally. Reduce the heat and simmer the chutney, uncovered, for about 1 hour. Stir occasionally during cooking to make sure that the chutney does not burn on the base of the pan.

Have ready some warmed jars with airtight lids. Spoon the hot chutney into the jars, top with waxed discs, placing the waxed side inwards, and cover immediately. Label and leave to cool before storing. The chutney will be ready to eat after a couple of weeks and, unopened, it will keep for 3 to 6 months. MAKES ABOUT 1.5 kg/3 lb.

BRAMBLE AND APPLE JAM

1 kg/2 lb cooking apples	1.75 kg/4 lb preserving sugar
300 ml/½ pint water	juice of 2 lemons
1 kg/2 lb blackberries	

PEEL, core and slice the apples. Put all the trimmings in a saucepan with the water and bring to the boil. Boil for 15 minutes, or until most of the water has evaporated.

Meanwhile, put the apples and blackberries in a large saucepan or preserving pan. Add about 225 g/8 oz of the sugar. Press the apple trimmings through a fine sieve to extract all the apple pulp and pectin from them. Add this to the fruit. Heat gently until the juice runs from the blackberries, then cook for 5 to 10 minutes, or until the apples are soft.

Add the remaining sugar to the pan and stir over a gentle heat until it dissolves completely. Stir in the lemon juice. Bring to the boil and boil hard until setting point is reached (see page 124).

Have ready warmed pots. Pour in the hot jam and cover with waxed discs, placing the waxed sides down. Allow to cool before covering the pots with cellophane tops or airtight lids. Label and store, unopened, for 6 to 9 months. MAKES ABOUT 3.25 KG/7 LB.

GREEN TOMATO AND APPLE CHUTNEY

450 g/1 lb cooking apples
1 kg/2 lb green tomatoes
450 g/1 lb onions
2 cloves garlic, crushed
2 green chillies
1 teaspoon ground ginger
1 teaspoon salt

½ teaspoon turmeric
¼ teaspoon ground cloves
50 g/2 oz sultanas
300 ml/½ pint vinegar
225 g/8 oz soft dark brown
  sugar

PEEL, core and roughly chop the apples. Put these in a large saucepan. Chop the green tomatoes and the onions and add to the apples with the garlic. Halve the chillies, carefully remove the seeds and cut off the stalks. Chop the green part and add to the pan with all the remaining ingredients.

Bring to the boil, stirring occasionally, then reduce the heat and simmer, uncovered, for about 1¼ to 1½ hours. At the end of the cooking time, the excess liquid should have evaporated and the chutney should be thick. Stir during cooking to make sure that the chutney does not stick to the base of the pan.

Have ready warmed pots. Spoon in the hot chutney and top with waxed discs, putting the waxed sides downwards. Cover with airtight lids while hot. Label and store, unopened, for up to 6 months. Allow the chutney to mature for 1 month before eating. MAKES ABOUT 1.75 KG/4 LB.

WINTER

IF you haven't already done so, then this is the time to make your Christmas puddings and cakes. For a change try a Dundee cake instead of a thickly iced traditional cake. You will also find a recipe for Pressed Tongue in this chapter – a traditional favourite for the festive cold table and it's easy enough to prepare, requiring only a little extra time. To continue the celebrations, why not make some Potted Stilton with home-made Oatcakes and a Warming Punch for New Year's Eve?

For all those day-to-day meals try making pot roasts, hotpots and dumplings. Or be adventurous and make a spicy Chilli Pork, exotic Lamb Curry or economical Cabbage Risotto. Remember that this is the season for Seville oranges, so stock up home-made marmalade too. For those times when you feel like doing some baking you could always try the Savoury Soda Bread, Chocolate Coconut Buns or delicious Crumpets – they're bound to cheer up a simple wintry tea.

COCK-A-LEEKIE SOUP

2 large chicken joints (preferably wing and breast joints)	salt and pepper
	1.75 litres/3 pints water
	few sprigs parsley
25 g/1 oz butter	450 g/1 lb leeks
1 medium onion, chopped	1 large potato
bay leaf	

SELECT meaty chicken joints. Alternatively, use the carcass of a roast chicken with plenty of meaty remains on it. A boiling fowl is ideal but you will have to increase the cooking time to 3 hours, or until the bird is thoroughly tender, and top up the liquid as it cooks.

Melt the butter in a large saucepan, add the onion and bay leaf and cook until the onion is soft but not browned. Add the seasoning and the chicken joints, then the water and parsley. Bring to the boil, cover and simmer for 45 minutes.

Meanwhile, slice the leeks and dice the potato. Remove the chicken from the pan, discard the skin and cut all the meat off the bones. Cut the meat into small pieces and return these to the soup. Add the leeks and potato and bring to the boil. Simmer, uncovered, for about 30 minutes, or until the leeks are cooked and the soup is reduced to about half the original quantity. Serve with warmed, crusty bread rolls. SERVES 4 TO 6.

BEEF SOUP

450 g/1 lb stewing beef	bay leaf
2 large onions	25 g/1 oz pearl barley
225 g/8 oz carrots	1.75 litres/3 pints water
1 large potato	2 tablespoons concentrated
1 small swede	tomato purée
salt and pepper	Croûtons to serve (page 125)

CUT all the fat off the meat and put the trimmings in a heavy-based sauce pan over a low heat until the fat runs. Press the trimmings occasionally to extract all the fat. Do not heat too quickly or the fat will burn. When the trimmings are dried out and crisp, press well and remove from the pan using a slotted spoon. Reserve the fat.

Finely dice the beef, chop the onions and dice the carrots, potato and swede. Fry the beef quickly in the reserved fat until browned on all sides, then use a slotted spoon to remove it from the pan. Fry the onions in the same fat over a moderate heat until browned. Stir frequently to prevent the onions sticking.

Add the beef, seasoning and bay leaf, then the pearl barley, water and tomato purée. Bring to the boil. Reduce the heat, cover and simmer gently for 3 hours, or until the barley is cooked and the soup reduced to about two-thirds of the original quantity.

Add the carrots, potato and swede and simmer for a further 30 minutes, or until the vegetables are tender.

Ladle the soup into warmed bowls and top each portion with Croûtons. Serve hot. SERVES 4 TO 6.

PORK PÂTÉ

450 g/1 lb pig's liver	½ teaspoon ground mace
2 onions	50 g/2 oz fresh breadcrumbs
50 g/2 oz butter	2 tablespoons brandy
2 large cloves garlic, crushed	150 ml/¼ pint full-bodied red wine
450 g/1 lb lean, boneless pork	salt and pepper
	4 bay leaves

CHOP the liver and onions. Melt the butter in a frying pan, add the garlic and liver and cook over a low heat until the liver is sealed. Stir in the onions and cook until softened. Remove from the heat.

Finely chop the pork, then mix it with the liver. Add the mace, breadcrumbs, brandy, wine and plenty of seasoning. Stir well to make sure that all the ingredients are thoroughly combined.

Grease an ovenproof terrine or dish (about 900-ml/1½-pint), then spoon in the pâté and press down well. Arrange the bay leaves on top and cover with a lid or foil. Stand the dish in a roasting tin and pour in boiling water to come up to the edge of the tin. Bake in a moderate oven (160 C, 325 F, gas 3) for 2 hours.

Remove the dish from the water bath and allow to cool for about 1 hour. Uncover, place a double thickness of foil over the pâté and weight it down. Leave until completely cold, then chill for a few hours before serving.

Lift off the weights and serve the pâté straight from the dish with French bread or hot toast. Some scrubbed celery, tomatoes and other salad vegetables also complement this pâté. SERVES 8.

MUSHROOM AND BACON KEBABS

24 button mushrooms
12 rashers rindless lean
(streaky) bacon

1 tablespoon sage and onion
mustard
8 bay leaves

TRIM any long stalks from the mushrooms. Cut the bacon rashers in half and spread each piece with a little mustard. Wrap each mushroom in a piece of bacon, then thread them on to four metal skewers, adding two bay leaves to each skewer. Cook under a hot grill, turning once, until the bacon is crisp and brown. Serve with warmed French bread and a fresh green salad. SERVES 4.

HOT GARLIC AND HERB BREAD

100 g/4 oz butter
1 clove garlic, crushed
1 tablespoon chopped fresh
thyme
2 tablespoons chopped
parsley

1 tablespoon chopped fresh
oregano, lemon balm or
rosemary, or mixed herbs
salt and pepper
1 French loaf

CREAM the butter with the garlic and herbs. Season lightly. Cut the French loaf into slices, leaving them all attached at the base. Spread the herb butter between the slices, then press them back together. Spread any remaining butter over the top of the loaf. Wrap the bread securely in aluminium foil, then bake in a moderately hot oven (200 C, 400 F, gas 6) for about 15 to 20 minutes, until heated through. The butter melts and the crust becomes crisp during cooking.

Separate the slices and arrange them in a napkin-lined basket, then serve at once. SERVES 6 TO 8.

ROAST TURKEY

CALCULATE the cooking time for the turkey by weighing the stuffed bird and allowing 20 minutes per 450 g/1 lb, plus an extra 20 minutes.

To prepare the bird, make sure that the giblets are removed from the body cavity. If the bird is frozen, defrost thoroughly before stuffing. Allow at least 24 hours defrosting time in a cool place, longer if the bird is very large or if you are defrosting it in the refrigerator.

Scald the body cavity of the turkey, then drain thoroughly. Press the stuffing into the bird and tie the legs and wings securely in place. Rub the skin with a little salt and lay some fatty, streaky bacon across the top to prevent the breast meat from drying out.

Place in a roasting tin and cover with aluminium foil. Roast in a moderate oven (180 C, 350 F, gas 4). Remove the foil for the last 40 to 50 minutes, so that the skin becomes brown and crisp. Baste the bird during cooking and pierce any fat bubbles towards the end of the cooking time.

For very large birds (in the region of 9–11 kg/20–24 lb), reduce the cooking temperature to 160 C/325 F/gas 3 and increase the cooking time to 25 minutes per 450 g/1 lb, plus an extra 25 minutes.

CHESTNUT AND SAUSAGEMEAT STUFFING

2 medium onions	salt and pepper
450 g/1 lb chestnuts	100 g/4 oz rindless lean
2 tablespoons chopped fresh	(streaky) bacon
sage	450 g/1 lb pork sausagemeat
100 g/4 oz fresh bread-	150 ml/¼ pint brandy
crumbs	

FINELY chop the onions. Put the chestnuts in a saucepan and add water to cover. Bring to the boil, cook for 1 minute, then remove from the heat. Lift out the chestnuts using a slotted spoon. Slit and remove the shells while the chestnuts are still hot.

Mix the chestnuts with the onion, sage and breadcrumbs and season well. Chop the bacon, add to the chestnut mixture and stir in the sausagemeat and brandy. ENOUGH FOR A 4.5-KG/10-LB BIRD.

SAGE AND ONION STUFFING WITH APPLE

450 g/1 lb fresh breadcrumbs	4 medium onions
4 tablespoons chopped fresh	450 g/1 lb dessert apples
sage	about 250 ml/8 fl oz milk
salt and pepper	

MIX the breadcrumbs with the sage and plenty of salt and pepper. Finely chop the onions and add to the breadcrumbs. Peel, core and finely chop the apples, then mix them into the stuffing. Add enough milk to make the mixture moist, stirring well to combine all the ingredients. ENOUGH FOR A 4.5-KG/10-LB BIRD.

BOILED BACON WITH VEGETABLES

1 (1.5-kg/3-lb) bacon joint, soaked in cold water for about 2 hours	few sprigs parsley
	1 small cabbage
	6 medium potatoes
1 large onion	1 small swede or 2 large
2 large carrots	parsnips
bay leaf	

DRAIN the bacon joint, rinse it and place in a very large saucepan. Pour in enough water to cover, then bring to the boil. Remove from the heat, drain, discard the water and put the joint back in the pan.

Slice the onion and carrot and add them to the pan with the bay leaf and parsley. Pour in enough water to cover the joint, then bring slowly to the boil. Carefully skim off any scum which rises to the top of the water. (After 2 or 3 minutes cooking, all the scum will have been cleared away.) Cover and simmer for 1 hour.

Meanwhile, shred the cabbage, cut the potatoes in half and cut the swede or parsnips into chunks. Add the potatoes and swede or parsnip to the bacon. Add more water if necessary and cook for a further 15 minutes. Add the cabbage and simmer for 5 to 10 minutes, or until the root vegetables are cooked.

To serve, lift the bacon out of the pan, cut off the rind and carve the joint into thick slices. Lift out the vegetables, using a slotted spoon, and pile them into a warmed tureen. Ladle a little of the broth over them before serving. The broth can be served as a first course or it can be used as the base for another soup. Alternatively, the vegetables and broth can be ladled into large bowls to be served with the sliced bacon. SERVES 6.

POT-ROASTED BRISKET

1 (1.5-kg/3-lb) joint of brisket	bay leaf
1 large onion	salt and pepper
450 g/1 lb leeks	300 ml/½ pint water
450 g/1 lb turnips	300 ml/½ pint beer or red wine
450 g/1 lb carrots	2 tablespoons flour
6 medium potatoes	25 g/1 oz butter, melted
1 tablespoon oil	

MAKE sure that the brisket is firmly tied in a neat shape. Thickly slice the onion and leeks, cut the turnips and carrots into large chunks and quarter the potatoes.

Heat the oil in a very large flameproof dish. Add the meat and cook until brown all over, then remove it from the pan. Fry the onion briefly in the same oil, then stir in all the other vegetables. Add the bay leaf and plenty of seasoning. Pour in the water and bring to the boil. When it is just boiling, remove from the heat. Lay the beef on top of the vegetables and cover the dish. Cook in a moderately hot oven (190 C, 375 F, gas 5) for about 2–2½ hours, or until the meat is tender.

To serve, transfer the meat to a warmed serving platter. Lift out the vegetables using a slotted spoon. Pour the beer or wine into the pan juices and heat gently, stirring constantly. Beat the flour into the butter, then add knobs of this paste to this sauce. Bring to the boil, stirring constantly.

Serve the brisket carved into thin slices, with the sauce and the vegetables. SERVES 6.

NOTE: If you do not have a large flameproof dish, then brown the meat in a frying pan and transfer all the ingredients to a roasting tin. Cover with foil during cooking.

PRESSED TONGUE

1 pickled ox tongue	2 bay leaves
salt	1 large onion, quartered
1 tablespoon black	2 large carrots, halved
peppercorns	a few sprigs of parsley and
2 blades of mace	thyme

SOAK the tongue overnight in cold water. Drain and scrape the skin well, then wash thoroughly and put in a large saucepan. Add cold water to cover and all the remaining ingredients. Bring slowly to the boil, skim off any scum and reduce the heat. Cover and simmer very gently for 5 or 6 hours, topping up the water as necessary.

Lift out the tongue and remove the skin and any tiny bones or gristle. If the tongue has been cooked for long enough, this task is easy. Roll it up and place in a cake tin or soufflé dish, spoon in a little cooking liquid and weight down until cold. Chill overnight, still weighted, then turn out on to a serving plate.

Serve sliced, as part of a cold meat platter or on its own. Baked potatoes, bread and butter and salads can be served with the cold meat. Offer French or English mustard or creamed horseradish as accompaniments. SERVES 6 TO 12, DEPENDING ON SIZE.

BEEF WITH WALNUTS

675 g/1½ lb lean braising	300 ml/½ pint beer
steak	bay leaf
4 tablespoons flour	100 g/4 oz mushrooms
1 large onion	25 g/1 oz butter
pared rind of 1 orange	100 g/4 oz walnut halves
2 tablespoons oil	2 tablespoons chopped
salt and pepper	parsley
1 (425-g/15-oz) can chopped	
tomatoes	

CUT the meat into neat, bite-sized cubes. Toss them in the flour and set aside. Chop the onion and cut the orange rind into fine strips.

Heat the oil in a large, flameproof dish and cook the onion until soft but not browned. Add the meat and fry until browned, then add the orange rind and salt and pepper to taste. Add the tomatoes, beer and bay leaf and stir well. Bring slowly to the boil, cover and simmer gently for 1½ hours, or until the meat is very tender. If you prefer, put the dish in a moderate oven (180C, 350F, gas 4) for the same amount of time.

Towards the end of the cooking time add the mushrooms and stir well. Then melt the butter in a small pan and cook the walnuts gently until lightly browned. Add these to the beef casserole and stir well. Serve with noodles or creamed potatoes. SERVES 4.

PARSLEY DUMPLINGS

225 g/8 oz self-raising flour
generous pinch of salt
4 tablespoons chopped
    parsley

100 g/4 oz shredded suet
175 ml/6 fl oz water

SIFT the flour into a bowl with the salt, then stir in the parsley and suet. Gradually add the water to make a soft but not too sticky dough. Knead lightly, then divide the dough into eight pieces. Flour your hands and shape each piece into a neat, round dumpling.

Cook the dumplings on top of a casserole or hotpot, simmering gently for about 15 minutes, or until they are well-risen and glossy. Alternatively, they can be simmered in a pan of stock (beef or chicken) to serve with less moist casseroles. They can also be simmered in a pot of soup, to make a hearty meal. SERVES 4.

HARICOT LAMB HOTPOT

225 g/8 oz dried haricot
 beans
1 kg/2 lb neck of lamb,
 chopped into chunks
3 tablespoons flour
2 teaspoons mixed herbs
salt and pepper
1 large onion
225 g/8 oz carrots

4 celery sticks
1 tablespoon oil
300 ml/½ pint red wine or
 beer and 300 ml/½ pint
 water
bay leaf
3 tablespoons chopped
 parsley

SOAK the haricot beans in cold water overnight. Next day, drain them and pick out any bad ones.

Trim any excess fat from the lamb. Mix the flour with the herbs and plenty of salt and pepper, then use to coat the pieces of lamb. Roughly chop the onion and cut the carrots and celery into chunks.

Heat the oil in a large, heavy-based saucepan. Add the pieces of lamb and brown them all over (they will yield a lot of fat). Remove the meat from the pan and drain off the excess fat. Fry the onion in the remaining fat, then add any remaining flour and stir well. Cook for a minute, stirring constantly, then add the wine or beer and water, still stirring. Add the bay leaf, carrots and celery. Season lightly and replace the meat in the pan. Bring to the boil, then reduce the heat, cover and simmer for 45 minutes. Stir occasionally to prevent the ingredients from sticking.

Stir the beans into the hotpot, making sure that they are covered by the liquid. Bring back to the boil, then reduce the heat, cover and simmer very gently for a further 50 to 60 minutes, or until the beans are tender but still firm. Add the parsley just before serving.

Some warm crusty bread and robust red wine make excellent accompaniments for this warming, simple dish. SERVES 4.

LAMB CURRY

675 g/1½ lb lean, boneless leg
  or shoulder of lamb
2 tablespoons fresh root
  ginger, grated
2 cloves garlic, crushed
2 tablespoons ground
  coriander
2 tablespoons ground cumin
1 teaspoon chilli powder
150 ml/¼ pint natural yogurt
¼–½ teaspoon salt

2 large onions
50 g/2 oz ghee or butter
1 cinnamon stick
4 whole green cardamoms
1 (425-g/15-oz) can chopped
  tomatoes
300 ml/½ pint water
bay leaf
2 tablespoons chopped fresh
  coriander

TRIM any fat from the meat and discard. Cut the meat into
bite-sized cubes. Mix the ginger with the garlic, coriander,
cumin, chilli, yogurt and salt. Add this mixture to the meat
and mix well to coat. Cover and leave to marinate
overnight.

Finely chop the onions. Melt the butter or ghee in a
heavy-based saucepan or flameproof dish. Add the onions
and cook until soft but not browned. Add the cinnamon,
cardamoms, meat with all its marinade, tomatoes, water
and bay leaf and stir well. Bring slowly to the boil, then
cover and simmer for about 1 hour, or until the meat is
tender. Stir occasionally.

If there is a lot of excess liquid in the curry at the end of
the cooking time, boil for a few minutes to evaporate the
excess. Sprinkle with chopped coriander just before
serving.

Plain boiled rice, crisp poppadums and a hot lime pickle
or sweet mango chutney go well with this curry. SERVES 4.

SCALLOPED EGGS

1 kg/2 lb potatoes	75 g/3 oz matured Cheddar
50 g/2 oz butter	cheese
salt and pepper	pinch of paprika
1 small onion	1 tablespoon chopped
50 g/2 oz button mushrooms	parsley
4 hard-boiled eggs	
1 quantity Basic White	
Sauce (page 126)	

COOK the potatoes in boiling, salted water until tender, about 20 minutes. Drain thoroughly and mash with half the butter and a little salt and pepper. Leave to cool slightly, then pipe a border of mashed potato round the edge of four ovenproof dishes.

Finely chop the onion and thinly slice the mushrooms. Shell and halve the eggs. Melt the remaining butter in a small pan and cook the onion until thoroughly softened but not browned. Add the mushrooms and cook for 1 minute, then remove from the heat. Season and divide the mushroom mixture between the dishes. Lay the halved eggs on top.

Make the Basic White Sauce, then beat in most of the cheese and season. Coat the eggs with the sauce and sprinkle the remaining cheese on the top. Brown in a hot oven (220C, 425F, gas 7) for about 15 minutes, or until bubbling hot.

Garnish with a little paprika and some chopped parsley, then serve hot with crisp toast. SERVES 4.

Variation

Alternatively, the eggs can be coated in a tarragon sauce. Follow the method for Basic White Sauce (see page 126), using 25 g/1 oz butter, 20 g/¾ oz flour and 150 ml/¼ pint dry white wine to make a very thick sauce. Then remove from the heat and stir in 150 ml/¼ pint single cream.

Season to taste and add 2 tablespoons chopped fresh tarragon.

Use this sauce instead of the cheese sauce, sprinkling the top of the coated eggs with 1 or 2 tablespoons Parmesan cheese before browning.

CHILLI PORK

350 g/12 oz red kidney beans
1 large onion
225 g/8 oz rindless streaky
    bacon
2 large cloves garlic, crushed
450 g/1 lb pork, minced
1 tablespoon ground coriander

1 tablespoon ground cumin
1 tablespoon chilli powder
1 (425-g/15-oz) can tomatoes
600 ml/1 pint water
2 tablespoons concentrated
    tomato purée
salt and pepper

SOAK the kidney beans for 3 or 4 hours, or overnight. Drain and put in a saucepan with plenty of fresh water. Bring to the boil, then boil hard for 5 minutes. Reduce the heat, cover and simmer for 30 minutes.

Meanwhile, finely chop the onion and the bacon. Place both in a saucepan with the garlic and heat gently until the fat runs from the bacon. Cook, stirring occasionally, until the onion is soft but not browned. Add the pork, increase the heat and brown the meat. Stir in the spices and cook for 1 minute. Add the tomatoes, water, tomato purée and plenty of seasoning. Stir well and bring to the boil.

Drain the beans and add them to the meat mixture. Cover the pan and simmer for about 1 hour, or until the beans are tender. If there is a lot of liquid left in the pan at the end of the cooking time, boil for a few minutes to evaporate the excess.

Serve with cooked rice or crusty bread and a salad.
SERVES 4.

SPROUTS WITH BACON AND HAZELNUTS

1 kg/2 lb Brussels sprouts
225 g/8 oz rindless lean
   smoked bacon
25 g/1 oz butter

50 g/2 oz chopped hazelnuts
pinch of black pepper

TRIM the sprouts, then cook them in boiling, salted water for 3 minutes. Roughly chop the bacon.

Melt the butter in a saucepan, add the nuts and cook gently until they are lightly browned. Add the bacon and cook gently until lightly browned, then stir in the drained sprouts. Toss to combine the sprouts with the other ingredients. Add the black pepper and cover. Cook gently for 3 to 5 minutes. Serve at once. SERVES 4.

CREAMY VEGETABLE GRATIN

1 small cauliflower
100 g/4 oz pickling onions
225 g/8 oz carrots
225 g/8 oz parsnips
4 celery sticks
100 g/4 oz button
   mushrooms
1 quantity Basic White
   Sauce (page 126)

150 ml/¼ pint single cream
100 g/4 oz Cheddar cheese,
   grated
2 teaspoons prepared
   English mustard
salt and pepper
1 large egg, beaten
3 tablespoons dried
   breadcrumbs

BREAK the cauliflower into florets and cook in boiling, salted water for 3 to 5 minutes, depending on how you like your vegetables cooked. Peel the onions and cook them in boiling water for about 5 minutes. Cut the carrots, parsnips and celery into chunks and cook in boiling, salted water for 10 to 15 minutes, or until tender.

Mix all the drained vegetables in an ovenproof dish with the mushrooms.

Make the Basic White Sauce very thick by using 25 g/ 1 oz flour. Remove the pan from the heat and beat in the cream. Stir in most of the cheese and the mustard. Season, then beat in the egg. Pour this sauce over the vegetables.

Mix the reserved cheese with the breadcrumbs and sprinkle over the top. Bake in a moderately hot oven (200 C, 400 F, gas 6) for about 30 minutes, or until golden and bubbling on top.

Serve freshly cooked as an accompaniment to grilled meats, sausages or bacon rolls. Alternatively, serve the gratin on its own or with hot, buttered toast, to make a hearty supper dish. SERVES 4 TO 6.

PARSNIP BAKE

450 g/1 lb parsnips
salt and pepper
1 medium onion
50 g/2 oz butter
pinch of freshly grated
  nutmeg

100 g/4 oz Cheshire cheese,
  finely crumbled
2 tablespoons fresh breadcrumbs

CUT the parsnips into chunks and cook in boiling, salted water until tender, about 20 minutes.

Meanwhile, finely chop the onion. Melt the butter and fry the onion until soft but not browned. Add the nutmeg.

Drain and thoroughly mash the parsnips, then beat in the onion and butter. Add three-quarters of the cheese and seasoning to taste. Turn the mixture into a greased, ovenproof dish. Mix the remaining cheese with the breadcrumbs and sprinkle this over the top. Bake in a moderately hot oven (200 C, 400 F, gas 6) for 20 to 25 minutes, until golden on top. Serve as a supper dish, with grilled bacon or with grilled chicken or chops. SERVES 4.

GRATIN OF FENNEL WITH HAM AND TOMATOES

4 large bulbs of fennel	salt and pepper
1 large onion	*Topping*
225 g/8 oz cooked ham	75 g/3 oz fresh breadcrumbs
50 g/2 oz butter	100 g/4 oz Caerphilly,
1 clove garlic, crushed	Lancashire or
1 (425-g/15-oz) can chopped	Wensleydale cheese,
tomatoes	finely crumbled
4 tablespoons dry sherry	150 ml/¼ pint soured cream
4 tablespoons water	salt and pepper

TRIM the feathery leaves off the fennel and reserve them. Trim off any bruised stalks and discard, then cut the bulbs in half. Finely chop the onion and dice the ham.

Melt the butter in a flameproof gratin or casserole dish. Add the onion and garlic and cook until the onion is soft but not browned. Add the fennel, placing the cut sides down, and fry for 2 or 3 minutes. Turn the bulbs over to cook the other sides for 2 or 3 minutes, then carefully lift them out. Stir in the tomatoes, sherry, water and seasoning to taste. Add the ham, sprinkling it over the tomatoes. Remove the pan from the heat.

Arrange the pieces of fennel in the pan so that they are half in the sauce. Cover tightly with a double layer of aluminium foil or a close fitting lid and bake in a moderate oven (180C, 350F, gas 4) for 45 to 50 minutes, or until the fennel is tender.

For the topping, mix most of the breadcrumbs with the cheese and stir in the soured cream. Season to taste. Chop the reserved fennel leaves and stir them into the topping. Spoon this mixture over the fennel, then sprinkle the few reserved breadcrumbs on top. Increase the oven temperature to moderately hot (200C, 400F, gas 6) and

cook for 20 to 30 minutes, òr until golden. Serve at once.
SERVES 4.

Variations
Gratin of Celery: Substitute fresh celery hearts for the
fennel in the main recipe.
Cabbage Bake: Large wedges of cabbage taste good cooked
in this dish. Do not soften the cabbage first, but put the
wedges straight into the tomato mixture. Cook, covered,
for 20 minutes only, then continue as in the main recipe.

CABBAGE RISOTTO

2 tablespoons oil	600 ml/1 pint chicken stock
l large onion, chopped	225 g/8 oz cooked ham
1 green pepper, deseeded	225 g/8 oz tomatoes
and chopped	1 small cabbage, finely
2 cloves garlic, crushed	shredded
225 g/8 oz long-grain rice	salt and pepper

HEAT the oil in a large saucepan, add the onion, garlic and
pepper and cook until the onion is soft but not browned.
Stir in the rice and fry until the grains are transparent. Add
the chicken stock and bring to the boil, then cover and
simmer for 15 minutes.

Meanwhile, dice the ham. Put the tomatoes into a bowl
and cover with boiling water. Leave for 2 or 3 minutes,
then drain and peel them. Cut the peeled tomatoes into
eighths.

Add the ham, tomatoes and cabbage to the risotto,
stirring gently to avoid breaking up the rice. Season lightly
and cook for a further 5 to 10 minutes, or until the rice is
tender and most of the liquid has been absorbed. Serve
immediately. SERVES 4.

CHRISTMAS PUDDING

100 g/4 oz raisins
100 g/4 oz sultanas
100 g/4 oz currants
100 g/4 oz cooking dates
100 g/4 oz dried apricots
150 ml/¼ pint stout
6 tablespoons brandy or rum
2 tablespoons black treacle
100 g/4 oz soft dark brown
 sugar
grated rind and juice of 1
 orange

½ teaspoon ground cinnamon
½ teaspoon ground mixed
 spice
1 large carrot
1 large cooking apple
175 g/6 oz fresh
 breadcrumbs
100 g/4 oz shredded suet
1 large egg, beaten

THIS is best made two or three months in advance, and will keep for up to a year. Mix the raisins, sultanas and currants in a bowl. Finely chop the dates and apricots, add the vine fruits and pour in the stout. Stir in the brandy or rum, treacle, sugar, orange rind and juice and spices and mix well. Soak overnight or for up to 3 days, stirring occasionally.

Peel and grate the carrot. Peel, core and grate the apple. Mix both into the fruit with the breadcrumbs, suet and egg. The moist mixture should just bind together – if it seems dry, add a little extra stout.

Grease a 1.15-litre/2-pint pudding basin and press the mixture into it. Cover with a large circle of greased grease-proof paper, making a pleat in the middle to allow room for the pudding to expand. Wrap the basin securely in double-thick cooking foil, sealing all the edges together really well.

Steam the pudding for 6 hours, topping up the water. Allow to cool for a few hours, then remove the foil but leave the greaseproof paper in place. Wrap the basin tightly in fresh foil to keep all the moisture in, then leave the pudding to mature.

To serve, steam the pudding for a further 2 hours, wrapping it securely in foil first. SERVES 6 TO 8.

BRANDY SAUCE

25 g/1 oz cornflour
25 g/1 oz sugar

600 ml/1 pint milk
4–6 tablespoons brandy

MIX the cornflour with the sugar and a little milk to make a smooth paste. Heat the remaining milk over a low heat. Just before it boils, pour some on to the cornflour paste, stirring constantly. Add this mixture to the milk and heat gently, stirring constantly, until the sauce boils. Cook for 2 to 3 minutes, then remove the pan from the heat and stir in brandy to taste.

Serve freshly cooked. If the sauce has to be kept for some time before serving, cover the surface with a piece of buttered greaseproof paper to prevent a skin forming. Reheat gently, stirring constantly. SERVES 6.

BRANDY OR RUM CREAM

300 ml/½ pint double cream
2 or 3 tablespoons icing sugar

4 tablespoons brandy or rum

VERY lightly whip the cream, then stir in the icing sugar and brandy or rum. The cream should be thickened rather than stiff. Serve at once. SERVES 6.

BRANDY OR RUM BUTTER

100 g/4 oz unsalted butter
75 g/3 oz caster sugar
1 tablespoon icing sugar

4–6 tablespoons brandy or rum

CREAM the butter with the sugars until very pale, then beat in brandy or rum to taste. Serve with the Christmas pudding or with mince pies. The butter can be stored in an airtight container in the refrigerator for up to 3 weeks. SERVES 6.

APPLE BATTER PUDDING

4 medium cooking apples
few drops lemon juice
50 g/2 oz butter
grated rind of 1 orange
1 teaspoon ground
   cinnamon
25 g/1 oz raisins

Batter
100 g/4 oz plain flour
2 large eggs, beaten
300 ml/½ pint milk
50 g/2 oz soft light brown
   sugar

PEEL, core and halve the apples, then sprinkle them with lemon juice. Melt the butter in a frying pan or flameproof dish. Add the apples, rounded side down, and cook briefly until lightly browned. Turn them over and cook for 1 minute, then add the orange rind, cinnamon and raisins. Stir, then remove from the heat. Transfer the apples to a greased ovenproof dish, if necessary, scraping all the cooking juices over them.

To make the batter, sift the flour into a bowl. Make a well in the centre and add the eggs. Gradually beat in the milk, working in the flour to make a smooth batter. Beat well, then add the sugar. Pour the batter over the apples and bake in a moderately hot oven (190 C, 375 F, gas 5) for about 35 to 45 minutes, or until well puffed and golden. Serve at once. SERVES 4 TO 6.

HOT CHOCOLATE SOUFFLÉ

50 g/2 oz butter	2 tablespoons brandy
15 g/½ oz flour	50 g/2 oz caster sugar
2 tablespoons cocoa powder	3 large eggs, separated
150 ml/¼ pint milk	icing sugar for dusting
grated rind of 1 orange	whipped cream to serve

MELT the butter in a large saucepan. Add the flour and cocoa powder, cook for 1 minute, then add the milk, stirring vigorously. Bring to the boil, stirring constantly, to make a very thick sauce. Remove from the heat and beat in the orange rind, brandy and sugar. Beat in the egg yolks, then leave to cool slightly.

Whisk the egg whites until they are stiff but not dry. Stir 2 tablespoons of the egg whites into the warm chocolate mixture, then carefully fold in the rest. Turn the soufflé mixture into a greased 18-cm/7-in soufflé dish and bake in a moderately hot oven (200C, 400F, gas 6) for 30 to 35 minutes, until well risen and crusted on top. Dust with icing sugar and serve at once, with lightly whipped cream. SERVES 4.

APRICOT MINCEMEAT PIE

225 g/8 oz dried apricots
1 cinnamon stick
pared rind of 1 orange
600 ml/1 pint apple juice
450 g/1 lb mincemeat

1½ quantities Shortcrust
    Pastry (page 126)
milk to glaze
whipped cream to serve

PLACE the apricots, cinnamon stick, orange rind and apple juice in a bowl. Cover and leave to soak overnight. Next day drain off the apple juice. Roll out two-thirds of the Shortcrust Pastry and use to line a deep tart-plate or pie dish. Fill with the apricots first, then the mincemeat. Dampen the rim of the pastry with water or milk. Roll out the remaining pastry to make a lid, lift it over the mincemeat and press the edges of the pastry together to seal. Trim the edges and use the trimmings to decorate the top of the pie. Brush the top lightly with milk to glaze and make a small hole in the centre. Bake in a moderately hot oven (200 C, 400 F, gas 6) for 35 to 40 minutes, or until the pastry is cooked.

Serve hot or warm, with whipped cream or the apple brandy sauce (below). SERVES 4 TO 6.

APPLE BRANDY SAUCE: Blend the remaining apple juice from soaking the fruit with 1 tablespoon cornflour, 4 tablespoons brandy and 2 tablespoons sugar. Heat through to boiling point, stirring constantly, then boil for 1 to 2 minutes. Remove the pan from the heat and stir in 150 ml/ ¼ pint double cream. Heat gently for a minute without boiling, then serve.

CRUMPETS

225 g/8 oz strong white flour
1 teaspoon salt
1 teaspoon sugar
1 sachet easy-blend yeast
250 ml/8 fl oz lukewarm water

½ teaspoon bicarbonate of soda
100 ml/4 fl oz lukewarm milk
oil for cooking

SIFT the flour and salt into a bowl, then stir in the sugar and yeast. Make a well in the centre, add the water and gradually work in the flour to make a very thick batter. Cover and leave in a warm place until increased in size and frothy – about 1 to 1½ hours.

Stir the bicarbonate of soda into the milk, then gradually beat this into the batter. Leave, covered, in a warm place until frothy – about 20 to 30 minutes.

Heat a griddle and grease it well. Use well-greased crumpet rings or large, plain biscuit cutters to mould the batter into crumpets. Put the rings on the griddle and spoon in some of the batter, to about half way up the ring. Reduce the heat slightly and cook until the batter is set and the bubbles have burst on top. Carefully remove the rings and turn the crumpets over. Cook until lightly browned.

Serve at once, with plenty of butter. Alternatively, cook very lightly on the second side and leave to cool on a wire rack, then toast the light side when you want to eat them. The crumpets freeze well, and can be stored for up to 3 months. MAKES ABOUT 10.

DUNDEE CAKE

225 g/8 oz butter	175 g/6 oz self-raising flour
225 g/8 oz soft light brown sugar	$\frac{1}{2}$ teaspoon ground mixed spice
grated rind of $\frac{1}{2}$ lemon	100 g/4 oz currants
grated rind of 1 orange and juice of $\frac{1}{2}$ orange	100 g/4 oz sultanas
3 tablespoons brandy	175 g/6 oz raisins
4 eggs, beaten	100 g/4 oz cut mixed peel
175 g/6 oz plain flour	225 g/8 oz blanched almonds

LINE a 20-cm/8-in loose-bottomed, round cake tin with greased greaseproof paper. Tie a double-thickness band of newspaper round the outside of the tin.

Cream the butter with the sugar and fruit rinds until very pale and soft. Add the orange juice and brandy to the eggs. Mix the flours with the spice. In a separate bowl, mix all the fruit together. Add a little flour to the fruit and toss well. Chop about three-quarters of the nuts and add to the fruit.

Gradually beat the eggs into the butter mixture, adding a spoonful of flour occasionally to prevent the mixture from curdling. When the eggs are incorporated, fold in the flour. Lastly, fold in the fruit. Turn the mixture into the prepared tin and smooth the top with the rounded side of a dampened metal spoon.

Arrange the whole almonds on top of the cake and bake in a moderate oven (160 C, 325 F, gas 3) for about 3 hours. To test if the cake is cooked, insert a metal skewer into the centre. It should come out clean.

Allow the cake to cool in the tin for 30 minutes, then transfer to a wire rack to cool completely, leaving the greaseproof paper on to keep the cake moist. This cake is best when stored in an airtight tin for a few days. MAKES 1 (20-CM/8-IN) CAKE.

MINCE PIES

1 quantity Sweet Shortcrust
   Pastry (page 126),
   flavoured with the grated
   rind of 1 orange

450 g/1 lb mincemeat
milk to glaze

MAKE the Sweet Shortcrust Pastry, adding the orange rind to the flour. Roll out about two-thirds of the pastry thinly and cut out circles to line two 12-space patty tins.

Put a little mincemeat in each pastry case. Do not overfill or the pies will leak during cooking. Roll out the remaining pastry and cut slightly smaller circles to make lids. Dampen the edges of the lids with milk, then press them on the pies. Brush the tops with a little milk to glaze and bake in a moderately hot oven (200 C, 400 F, gas 6) for 20 to 25 minutes, or until golden.

Cool the pies on wire racks, then store them in an airtight container. Serve on their own or with brandy and whipped cream. MAKES ABOUT 24.

WARMING PUNCH

1 large orange
6 cloves
1 cinnamon stick
50 g/2 oz blanched almonds
50 g/2 oz raisins

2 tablespoons soft dark
   brown sugar
150 ml/¼ pint orange juice
150 ml/¼ pint rum or brandy
1 bottle red wine

STICK the orange with the cloves and place it in a saucepan. Add all the other ingredients. Leave to stand for about 30 minutes, or longer if possible, then slowly heat the punch, keeping the heat on the lowest setting. When the punch has had time to reach full flavour (about 30 to 45 minutes), serve very warm. SERVES 6.

CHOCOLATE COCONUT BUNS

100 g/4 oz butter or
  margarine
100 g/4 oz soft light brown
  sugar
2 eggs
100 g/4 oz self-raising flour

100 g/4 oz desiccated
  coconut
100 g/4 oz chocolate drops
  for cooking
2 tablespoons milk

CREAM the butter or margarine with the sugar until pale and very light. Beat in the eggs, adding a little of the flour to prevent curdling. Fold in the remaining flour, coconut and chocolate drops. Lastly, gently fold in the milk to soften the mixture.

Divide between about 20 greased patty tins and bake in a moderate oven (180 C, 350 F, gas 4) for about 15–20 minutes, or until risen and golden. Leave in the tin for a minute, then turn out on to a wire rack to cool. MAKES ABOUT 20.

SAVOURY SODA BREAD

450 g/1 lb wholemeal flour
1 teaspoon bicarbonate of
  soda
2 teaspoons salt
1 tablespoon dried mixed
  herbs

50 g/2 oz matured Cheddar
  cheese, grated
1 large onion, grated
300 ml/½ pint milk

MIX the flour, soda, salt, herbs and cheese in a large bowl. Stir in the onion, make a well in the middle and pour in the milk Mix to make a soft dough, then knead very briefly until smooth. Divide the dough in half and shape into two round loaves. Place on greased baking trays and cut a large cross in the top of each loaf. Bake in a moderately hot oven

(190 C, 375 F, gas 5) for 40 to 45 minutes, or until risen, brown and crusty on top. Cool on a wire rack and serve warm. MAKES 2 LOAVES.

OATCAKES

50 g/2 oz plain flour	1 teaspoon sugar
100 g/4 oz fine oatmeal	½ teaspoon bicarbonate of
40 g/1½ oz butter	soda
½ teaspoon salt	4 tablespoons water

SIFT the flour into a bowl. Add the oatmeal and rub in the butter. Stir in the salt and sugar and bicarbonate of soda. Gradually add the water to make a firm dough. Cut the dough in half and press it into a well-greased 25-cm/10-in sandwich tin. Mark the round into six or eight wedges, then bake in a moderate oven (180C, 350F, gas 4) for about 25 minutes, or until very lightly browned.

Leave the oatcakes to cool slightly in the tin, then transfer them to a wire rack to cool completely.

Serve buttered, with cheese. MAKES 6 TO 8.

POTTED STILTON

225 g/8 oz blue Stilton cheese	pinch of freshly ground black pepper
5 tablespoons port	

CRUMBLE the cheese, then mash it with the port and pepper. Press into a small dish or earthenware pot, cover tightly and chill for several days.

Serve with oatcakes, Bath Oliver biscuits or water biscuits. SERVES 6 TO 8.

SEVILLE MARMALADE

1 kg/2 lb Seville oranges	2.25 litres/4 pints water
2 lemons	1.75 kg/4 lb preserving sugar

PUT the oranges, lemons and water in a large pan. Bring to the boil, cover and simmer for about 2 hours, or until the fruit is tender. Leave, covered, until cool enough to handle.

Chop the fruit, discarding the pips, then return it to the pan. Add the sugar and heat gently, stirring occasionally, until the sugar has dissolved. Bring to the boil and boil hard until the marmalade begins to set. To test for setting, put a little marmalade on a very cold saucer, leave for a few minutes and then push it with your fingertip. There should be a distinctive skin on the surface, so that it wrinkles. If the marmalade does not set, boil a little longer – but be careful not to overcook it.

Leave the marmalade to stand for about 15 minutes, skimming the surface of any scum. Pour into warmed jars and cover with waxed discs, waxed side down. When cool, cover, label and store in a cool place. MAKES ABOUT 3.25 KG/7 LB.

TESTING FOR SETTING: To test for setting when making jams, jellies and marmalades, put a little of the preserve on a very cold saucer and leave to cool. As it cools, if the setting point is reached a skin will form on the surface and this will wrinkle when the preserve is gently pushed with one finger. Alternatively use a sugar thermometer – this should register 104 C/220 F when setting point is reached.

BASIC RECIPES

CHICKEN STOCK

PUT a meaty chicken carcass or a large chicken joint in a large saucepan. Add a quartered onion and carrot, a bay leaf and a blade of mace. Pour in water to cover and bring to the boil. Cover and simmer for 2 hours. Strain, remove any meat from the bones and cut up to return to the stock. Season and use as required.

MELBA TOAST

TOAST medium-thick slices of bread. Working quickly, cut off the crusts and slice each piece of toast horizontally to give very thin pieces. Toast the uncooked sides. When cooled, melba toast can be stored in an airtight container for several days.

CROÛTONS

CUT medium-thick slices of brown or white bread into small even cubes. Melt about 25 g/1 oz butter in 2–3 tablespoons oil, then fry the bread cubes in the hot fat, turning frequently, until evenly browned. Drain on absorbent kitchen paper and serve as required.

BASIC WHITE SAUCE

MELT 25 g/1 oz butter in a saucepan, stir in 40 g/1½ oz flour
and cook gently, stirring, for a minute. Gradually pour in
600 ml/1 pint milk, stirring all the time. Bring to the boil,
still stirring, and cook for 2–3 minutes. Season to taste.

Cheese Sauce: Stir 75–100 g/3–4 oz grated cheese and 1–2
teaspoons made English mustard into the sauce.
Egg Sauce: Stir 4 chopped hard-boiled eggs into the sauce.
Add a little chopped tarragon or parsley.
Parsley Sauce: Add 4 tablespoons chopped parsley to the
sauce.
Mushroom Sauce: Add 225 g/8 oz sliced button mush-
rooms to the sauce and cook gently for a few minutes.
Onion Sauce: Finely chop 1 large onion and soften it in the
butter. Continue as above.

SHORTCRUST PASTRY

PUT 225 g/8 oz plain flour and pinch of salt in a bowl. Add
100 g/4 oz fat (margarine or half and half margarine and
lard) cut into pieces. Rub the fat into the flour until the
mixture resembles breadcrumbs. Add 2–3 tablespoons cold
water and lightly mix the pastry crumbs together.

SWEET SHORTCRUST PASTRY

MAKE as above, using 225 g/8 oz plain flour, 175 g/6 oz
butter or margarine, adding 25 g/1 oz caster sugar. Bind
with 1 egg yolk and chill until required.

Index